Reacting to the Past
Game Designer's Handbook

Nicolas W. Proctor
Simpson College

Third Edition
May 2013

Introduction

Games were what originally interested me in history. A boyhood spent playing hex-based historical games with my uncle and grandfather encouraged me to develop the notion that history is not so much a record of things said and done as it is a series of high stakes decisions.

When I started teaching, I took this idea with me into the classroom, where I experimented with modified versions of games like *Diplomacy* and *SIMSOC*. I also developed games of my own including text-based historical role-playing games, tabletop battles with military miniatures, an online crisis simulation, and various short role-playing exercises. Through trial and error, these efforts taught me a great deal about game design.

When I first discovered Reacting to the Past (RTTP) in 2001, I was surprised and gratified to find another instance of gaming in the humanities. I attended my first Reacting conference in 2005, and I was suffused with joy – *there were other people like me!* Soon though, I became depressed; I realized that their games were better, bigger, and more ambitious than mine. I swallowed my pride, regained my equilibrium, and began incorporating RTTP into my classes. Soon afterwards, I shifted most of my game design efforts towards RTTP.

For many instructors, RTTP represents their first exposure to game-based pedagogy, and in many ways, RTTP *is* revolutionary, but we must recognize that it is not alone in its use of games to teach important things. Military and policy games and simulations have been around for decades. Game theory is an established field of mathematics, and largely thanks to the electronic gaming industry, game design has become an academic discipline in its own right. The work of scholars and professionals in these fields is complemented by designers of new sports, serious games, pervasive games, augmented reality games, role-playing adventure games, and street games. Consequently, useful scholarship about game design is rapidly increasing. This handbook represents my efforts to bring some of this scholarship together with my experience as a RTTP instructor, playtester, and designer.

I self-published the first edition of this handbook in May 2011. The second edition included significantly more material, much of which came from discussions in the Facebook group "Reacting to the Past: Faculty Lounge," as well as my experience teaching a game design seminar, reviewing games in development, continuing work on my own designs, and serving as the chair of the RTTP Editorial Board.

In addition to those resources, this third edition benefitted from a research trip I took in the spring of 2013 to visit RTTP classrooms at a number of different institutions. My conversations with faculty, students, and administrators greatly expanded my understanding of how RTTP works in a wide variety of institutions. The same spring, I conducted a survey of students in RTTP classes. This also helped to shed light on the variety of ways in which the games are actually used.

As a result, in addition to a number of textual refinements and additions, this edition includes chapters on scalability (designing games so that they can be used in as many ways as is possible) and chapter games (shorter versions of RTTP). These seemed particularly important to think about because many faculty members have such a difficult time adapting full-length games to fit their classes.

When providing examples in the text below, I draw upon published games as often as possible, but I also mention a number of unpublished games. In these cases, the games have been heavily playtested and are available either from the author (who, in these cases, I list) or from the online RTTP Game Library.

Nicolas W. Proctor
Des Moines, Iowa
May 2013

Table of Contents

1. Series Standards

Once one grasps the essential elements of any game, it becomes easy to grasp other games with similar structures. For example, once you learn one card game, you understand the basic materials and systems of interaction, so others are fairly easy to pick up. If you know how to play Go Fish then Gin Rummy comes fairly easily. On the other hand, expertise in card games is not good preparation for Chess. Transitioning from one sort of game to another requires effort. If you must learn an entirely new set of rules and interactions every time you want to play a new game, you end up spending more time learning *how* to play than you do actually playing the game. Consequently, there are shared conventions to the RTTP series. This facilitates easy adoption by instructors and quick orientation for students who have played other games in the series. Every RTTP game includes the following elements: [1]

Real historical setting. RTTP games are set in the past, and players become oriented to the past world they will inhabit in the game through several opening days of traditional instruction. The setting must facilitate a meaningful and informed exchange of diverse ideas from a variety of points of view.

---

[1] These standards were determined by the Reacting Consortium Board in 2011.

Rich texts. Growing out of the Columbia University Great Books curriculum, the first collection of games developed by Mark Carnes feature Plato's *Republic,* Confucius' *Analects,* and the *Bible* as key sources. RTTP games now include texts from outside the canon, including collections of documents and works from the visual and performing arts, but every game remains firmly grounded in exceptionally rich historical source material.

Multiple meetings. Most games require around ten sessions. In most cases, the first two or three are devoted to traditional instruction and initial player meetings to set up the game, while at least one final session is devoted to debriefing and reflection.

Roles with well-developed characters. Players receive historical personas with objectives to achieve and ideas to advance. Roles require players to promote various interpretations of the key texts that accompany every game. The pursuit of these objectives and the expression of these ideas enmeshes players in the game, which leads to significant ***emotional investment.*** Engaging texts, arguments, and other players immerses players in their roles to the degree that games often take on ***elements of liminality.***[2]

Victory objectives. The roles must include victory objectives for players to pursue. Players who achieve their victory objectives win the game. Each player must begin with an idea on how he or she could achieve victory.

Intellectual collisions. Roles need to be placed in intellectual opposition, so they can debate the merits of various interpretations

---

[2] For more on RTTP and liminality, see Mark Carnes, "Being There: The Liminal Classroom," *Chronicle Review* (Oct. 8, 2004).

of the texts. The interplay of ideas in historical context with the competing objectives of the players drive the games forward. There must be multiple collisions.

Indeterminacy. Some roles must be undecided or "indeterminate" on some of the issues. The opportunity to persuade these players gives life to the intellectual collisions at the center of every game.

Reading, writing and speaking. Players must engage the texts on several levels. First, they must read them. Then, they must write persuasive speeches, articles, or essays about them. Finally, they must use these writings as a foundation for their spoken attempts to persuade other players to adopt their interpretations of the texts. In doing these things, players improve their abilities to make arguments and their ability to critique arguments made by others.

Narrative structure with drama. Changing the terms of player interactions prevents the game from ossifying into a static debate. Some of these interactions change as players deepen their understanding of the ideas that drive the game, but providing announcements that alter the parameters of the game ensures that players need to rethink old positions and/or conceptualize approaches to new problems.

Possibilities for alternate historical outcomes. It must be possible for player actions to have an impact on the outcome of the game. Empowering players in this way may result in historically inaccurate outcomes. However, if games lack this possibility, they cease to function as games and become, in essence, reenactments.

Accessibility to non-specialists. RTTP games must be able to stand alone. Players lacking background knowledge must be able to play.

Furthermore, Game Masters (GMs) must be able to run games that fall outside their areas of expertise.

The following elements are often incorporated into RTTP designs, but they are not necessarily integral to the pedagogy.

Factions. Many games clump roles together into factions. They function as small learning communities, which provide welcome emotional support as well as sounding boards for their developing ideas about the intellectual collisions that drive the game.

Elements of secrecy. It can be useful to keep some objectives for some roles concealed. This adds intrigue. It also helps prevent the debate from locking up.

Opening vignettes. Most games include a short, first-person piece of historical fiction at the beginning of the gamebook. These help orient players to the issues, tone, and setting.

Central text(s). Many games focus the players on the intellectual collisions within a single (often canonical) text.

RTTP games are designed for use by undergraduates, and they are used in different formats and configurations throughout the higher education. Students appear in these classes for all sorts of reasons. Consider the variety of answers expressed by students in an online survey I conducted in the spring of 2013. Around 300 students from sixteen colleges and universities of varying sizes and configurations responded to fifteen questions using Surveymonkey. RTTP aficionados may be overrepresented, but several faculty members trooped their classes to computer labs in order to get full coverage.

What's the approximate size of your class?

Less than 15	20 %
16-20	38 %
21-25	34 %
26+	7 %

How many RTTP games were part of this course?

One	58 %
Two	24 %
Three	18 %

Before taking this course, how many RTTP games had you played?

None	76 %
One	8 %
Two or more	11 %
So many I've lost count	6%

What is your primary reason for taking this course?
(Check all that apply)

First year seminar	18 %
General Education	40 %
Academic major	35 %
You get to play a game	26 %
Interesting subject	48 %
Convenient time slot	16 %

Regardless of where they fall in the curriculum, RTTP create excitement, engagement, and energy. This encourages instructors to use the games in all sorts of formats and for a variety of purposes. So, in addition to adhering to the series standards, the games must be flexible enough to be modified by the instructors who end up using them.

If you think your idea for a game can cohere to these standards and you a prepared to work on it over a long period of time, contact me at nick.proctor@simpson.edu and I will let you know how to register your idea with the RTTP Editorial Board.

2. Conceptualization

Take a moment to consider the resources that are available to you for developing the game. Researching, designing, writing, playtesting, and revising a good RTTP game takes years of work. Learning how to design a game requires developing expertise in a new genre of historical writing. You might brainstorm the basic structure quite quickly, but once you start developing the game, you will find that the interlocking elements require careful writing, thoughtful design, and a surprising amount of research (even if you already know the topic well). Since games include multiple, carefully balanced elements, revisions often necessitate a cascade of changes. All this is a way of saying: it is harder than you think.

Furthermore, playtesting ends up being more time consuming than other methods of academic peer review. Playtests must be scheduled for classes and conferences well in advance, so you often find yourself in a cycle of "hurry up and wait" as you make needed revisions in time for book orders only to be put on pause as months pass before a new semester begins.

This is a necessary evil because you must plan on repeatedly playtesting your design in your own courses, as well as providing remote assistance and support for numerous field tests at other institutions. In addition, you will need to run an abridged version of the game at conferences. So, this is a long haul. Is it worth it? Of course it is.

In order to get off to a good start, it is essential to be as specific as possible about your learning objectives. This is a critical first step. Game designer Cathy Stein Greenblat insists,

> This stage is too often skipped or undertaken casually, and the world-be designer's initial enthusiasm is translated into only a vague formulation such as 'I want to design a game about local politics,' with no thought given to what the gaming-simulation is supposed to convey, to whom, and under what conditions of play. The result is often total failure or a product that is totally inappropriate for the intended audience.[3]

In an effort to avoid these grim outcomes, clarify your learning objectives by developing answers to the following questions:

When and where will your game be set? Consult the Big List of Reacting Games (the BLORG), which is on the RTTP website, to see if there are any other games in development that overlap or complement your idea. If so, contact their designers and the Editorial Board.

What ideas will your game focus upon? In addition to material about a specific time and place, most RTTP games also address "big questions" like, what are the tensions between faith and reason?

What will players read? Players need to understand the intellectual basis of the arguments they will make in the course of a game, so they need interesting and fairly accessible historical documents

---

[3] Cathy Stein Greenblat, *Designing Games and Simulations: An Illustrated Handbook* (Newbury Park, CA: Sage Publications, 1987), 27.

that relate to their positions. Every ideological position that is present in the game should be supported by documents.

Are there multiple issues in contention? In order to function as a game, the structure of RTTP requires the potential for shifting coalitions. If there is only one issue, it often ossifies into a debate. On each issue, a broad spectrum of disagreement is ideal.

Are there interesting people involved in these debates? Identify individuals and institutions that were (or could have been) major factors in determining the outcome of significant events in the setting for your game. [4] Also look for people who developed particularly strong ideological positions. Initially, throw all of the possible roles you can think of into the mix.

Also ask yourself, which roles seem like they would be fun and interesting to play? Instead of saddling a player with an uninteresting or static role, try to fold it into the game mechanism or incorporate aspects of it into an existing role. For example, *The Threshold of Democracy: Athens in 403 B.C.* may feature intervention by Persia, but there is no Persian player. Instead, there is a chart that the GM may consult if a player makes the decision to initiate diplomatic negotiations.

How do the roles interact? Players will interact intellectually by giving speeches and asking questions. In some ways, these interactions are fairly typical of college classrooms, but they deepend and intensify when they take place within a role-playing game.

To begin thinking of the relationship between players in this way, consider the resources available to them. These can vary quite widely. They might include things like troops, votes,

---

[4] Greenblat, 62-63.

prestige, money, or information. The exchange of these resources is managed through the game mechanism.

Most game mechanisms are mathematical. If you attempt to model complicated historical events like wars, elections, or migrations, this may appear reductionist, but the clean simplicity of mathematics is a good thing for a game because it makes the system easy to understand for players and GMs.

Simple arithmetic does not detract from the complicated interactions that lie on top of it. Consider games as different as Chess, Gin Rummy, and American Football. Each of these games requires fairly simple mathematics in order to operate, but we do not usually perceive them as "math games." A simple mathematical system at the heart of your game does not make it a game about math, nor does it made the outcome easy to predict.

Given the complexity of the past, it is tempting to create byzantine clockworks with sophisticated and nuanced mechanisms that model multiple systems. However, an extensive set of systems requires an extensive set of rules, and if players do not understand the rules that govern a game, they cannot engage it in a meaningful way; instead of grappling with ideas, they spend their time trying to figure out the rules. Avoid the trap of thinking that complex games require complex systems. As game designer Raph Koster notes, "the intricacies of games come from either having a lot of mechanics or having a few, very elegantly chosen ones."[5] Choose the second path.

The core of your game mechanism is your *primary system*. It regulates the use of the main resource your players possess. This might sound complicated. It is not. In most cases, the primary system is very simple. In most games the "resource" is votes and the primary system is the casting and counting of those votes. Governed by simple arithmetic, such a system is a snap to operate.

---

[5] Raph Koster, *A Theory of Fun for Game Design* (Scottsdale: Paraglyph Press, 2005), 120.

To make this work, simplicity must be accompanied by precision. Unlike a book where the reader is pulled along by the narrative despite possible misconceptions or oversights, the non-linear nature of games means that, as wargame designer James Dunnigan puts it, "minor mistakes or ambiguous passages that might not seriously harm a nonfiction work can cause grave problems in a game."[6] This is an unforgiving medium.

Precision is essential because but before a system can begin to function, players must understand its operation. Voting is a good choice because the basics of such systems are intuitively grasped by players. No special training is required to vote, and they are easily cast. If players understand how to use the primary system, they can enter the game without delay. Therefore, its purpose and function must be clear. Players need to know what the system is for, how it operates, and how to interact with it.

Keep in mind that the game mechanism is a means to an end. Its function is to provide a matrix for player interaction. As such, when designing one, you should prioritize functionality over accurately modeling historical reality. For example, *Kentucky, 1861,* collapses two houses of the Kentucky state legislature into one while eliminating a variety of historical processes (committees, arcane procedures, multiple houses, etc.). This is because the objective of the game is to create an arena for the collision of ideas about loyalty and secession. If the objective was to accurately simulate the functioning of the Kentucky state legislature it would be a very different game.

After designing the primary system of your game mechanism, figure out what other things potential connect the roles. What other resources do they possess and how to they relate to the primary

---

[6]James F. Dunnigan, *The Complete Wargames Handbook*, 2nd Edition, 1997. Now online at:
http://www.hyw.com/Books/WargamesHandbook/Contents.htm.

system? The use of these resources usually compliments the primary system, so I refer to them as *secondary systems.*

Although adding additional systems makes your game mechanism more complex, there are virtues to including secondary systems in your design. These allow for more accurate historical modeling, but perhaps more importantly, they make the game is dynamic and unpredictable (i.e. fun). For example, in *Confucianism and the Succession of the Wanli Emperor, 1587,* the primary system of voting is complemented by a secondary system of bribery, which shows the power of the First Grand Secretary and adds an element of palace intrigue. It also complicates the fairly simple arithmetic governing the final vote. If properly deployed, a bribe can shift the outcome of the game.

Unlike the primary system, secondary systems need not be fully understood by all of the players. It may even be important to keep a secondary system concealed from some of them. However, if a secondary system begins to alter the functioning of the primary system or the fate of particular players, it should be revealed to everyone.

Finally, do not forget that while players may possess incomplete understanding of the secondary systems, the GM must understand them all, so fully describe their function, timing, and reason for existing in the Instructor's Manual (IM). So, keep one eye on playability.

Rousseau, Burke, and the Revolution in France, 1791, provides a good example of a primary system that interacts with the phased introduction of secondary systems. Together, these systems compose the game mechanism.

Primary system: Voting in the National Assembly
Understood by: Everyone
Frequency of use: Every session
Complexity: Simple at first, but Crowd Action complicates it

Secondary system: Crowd Action
Understood by: The Crowd and Lafayette
Frequency of use: 3-4 times, but not in the first session
Complexity: It's pretty complex. There are tables and such
Influence on primary system: Alters the number of votes

Secondary system: Invasion
Understood by: Inchoate understanding by a few, which takes
    clearer form as the game progresses
Frequency of use: Once, at the end of the game
Complexity: Simple. It's resolved by a modified die roll

In this game, like most, the primary system comes into play during the first session. Initially, almost every role has the same number of votes to cast, so once a resolution is called to a vote, it is an easy system to understand. Crowd Action is prohibited during the first session, so everyone has the opportunity to become comfortable with the primary system before the secondary system comes into play. Players see how other players vote, so they begin developing an understanding of where other roles fall on the issues. This also gives the GM a chance to make sure people understand their roles.

Then, once Crowd Action begins, players clearly see how it interacts with the primary system: People start to die. This shifts the weight of different players' votes. All of this is a neat little package because the secondary system loops back so tightly. The impact of the operation of the secondary system is reflected by changes in the primary system. Thus, most players never really need to understand how the mathematics of Crowd Action works; they can stay focused on the ideas that it represents.

The invasion of France by counter-revolutionary forces potentially occurs during the final session of the game. The functioning of this system, which is largely managed by the GM, determines the end state of the game with a die roll, which is modified by the resolutions that emerged from voting in the National Assembly (primary system), the bloodletting by the Crowd (secondary system), and the actions of the king. The ability to shift the odds is important because it lets players know that the decisions they made during the game were important ones.

It can be difficult to keep track of your game mechanism. Creating a visual representation can be a good tool for developing a fuller understanding of how it functions, so consider creating an organizational chart or concept map for each system and then show how they interact.[7] Make sure that you use a big piece of paper because even simple games feature multiple feedback loops and interconnections between different elements.

Some of the connections between various game elements are obvious, but others are subtle, so it is a good idea to update your chart regularly as your game develops. If you don't do this, you may lose track of all your interconnections, and forget how some components relate to one another. When it comes time for playtesting, you will thank yourself for sketching this out at the outset. It greatly simplifies things when you start adjusting different components of your game. It is also helpful in terms of defining the objectives and responsibilities attached to different roles.

Why a game? The final question is the hardest. What is it about the interaction of texts, players, and systems that makes your game into a powerful learning tool? Why will devoting a substantial amount of time to playing your game be more instructive than

---

[7] The concept map for the *Darwin* game is online at:
http://www.darwingame.org/Darwin%20Game%20Cmap.html

reading a book, attending a lecture, watching a film, using a website, or participating in a traditional discussion?

Your answer probably has something to do with interactivity, competition, cooperation, immersion, liminality, and fun because these are hallmarks of RTTP, but it is helpful to break this down into an explanation geared towards a peer who lacks experience with the series. You will be called upon to explain why you are putting so much time and energy into writing a *game,* so the more you think about your answer now, the better you will be able to articulate it later. Ideally, keeping this question foremost in your mind will also inform the structure and contents of your game.

3. Introducing Players to the Game

RTTP games are tools for learning, but designers must not lose sight of the fact that they are also *games*. If they do not work as games, they will not work as instruments for instruction.

This chapter draws heavily upon current scholarship about game design. Those who are inspired to learn more should consult Tracy Fullerton, *Game Design Workshop: A Playcentric Approach to Creating Innovative Games,* 2nd ed., Katie Salen and Eric Zimmerman, *Rules of Play: Game Design Fundamentals,* and Raph Koster, *A Theory of Fun for Game Design.* All of these books emphasize electronic gaming, but they are well grounded in game design in general. I've tried to bring their most salient ideas into this text.

When exploring the structure of various game mechanisms, these designers maintain focus on the ultimate goal of any game: *meaningful play*. Salen and Zimmerman describe this as something that "emerges from the interaction between players and the system of the game, as well as from the context in which the game is played."[8]

Achieving this on a superficial level is fairly easy. At the beginning of a game, players chat contentedly with one another and, if you have designed an intuitive primary system, they happily cast a vote or two without much prompting. While this can lead to

---

[8] Katie Salen and Eric Zimmerman, *Rules of Play: Game Design Fundamentals* (Cambridge, London: MIT Press, 2004)*,* 33.

a pleasant series of interactions, they do not carry a great deal of intellectual weight, which can make it difficult to achieve your learning objectives. In order to become *meaningful*, the interactions between players and the game mechanism must be informed by the game's historical context, by the texts that you have selected for them to read, and by the actions of other players. Amicable conversation can be a fine beginning, but it must deepen and intensify.

The Magic Circle

Game theorist Johan Huizinga writes engagingly about the ability of games to draw a "magic circle" around the participants. By playing, they step into a place apart from their ordinary realities.[9] The cry "play ball," the shuffling of a deck of cards, or a cut-scene from *Grand Theft Auto* all signal the creation of a special, temporary reality. Tracy Fullerton describes the liberation that comes from stepping into this circle,

> Bound by the rules of play, we perform actions that we would never otherwise consider—shooting, killing, and betrayal are some. But we also perform actions we would like to think ourselves capable of and have never had the chance to face—courage in the face of untenable odds, sacrifice, and difficult decision making.[10]

Describing the same phenomenon, game designer and theorist Mary Flanagan notes, "Play traverses ordinary life and allows

---

[9] Salen and Zimmerman, 94-99.

[10] Tracy Fullerton, *Game Design Workshop: A Playcentric Approach to Creating Innovative Games,* 2nd ed. (Burlington, MA: Elsevier Press, 2008), 49.

players to take on difficult issues from an insulated position."[11] This precisely describes what becomes possible in an RTTP classroom. Players are given gives permission to engage in spirited, high stakes debate and skullduggery while being insulated from the harsh consequences that often attend vigorous engagement in "real life." In order to achieve this level of engagement, games must immerse players in a different world.

Help draw the Magic Circle by altering the physical space in which the game takes place. Most games take place in a stylized space that sets it apart from ordinary reality. Playing fields, game boards, and high resolution graphics all create special spaces. In the case of an RTTP classroom, the GM should become unobtrusive, and may withdraw to the back of the room. Provide advice on rearranging the players too. Exalt elites with preferential seating. Have factions sit together (provided these alliances are public knowledge), and put socially marginalized roles on the edges of the classroom. Alternatively, if everyone is equal, jumble them up in markedly informal seating arrangements.

By using the space to encourage certain kinds of interactions while discouraging others, these arrangements signal the presence of factions and hierarchies. This helps define the Magic Circle. When the classroom becomes a space for play, new thoughts and action become possible.

Such rearrangements should visibly reinforce the functioning of the game mechanism. When players enter the room they remember: something different happens here. Then, by examining the arrangement, they can begin to understand much of what that different thing is. Like many games, *The Trial of Anne Hutchinson: Liberty, Law and Intolerance in Puritan New England* uses voting as its primary system, but not everyone gets to vote. The disfranchised must sit outside the circle of those who possess

---

[11] Mary Flanagan, *Critical Play: Radical Game Design* (Cambridge, London: MIT Press, 2009), 192.

church membership. Thus, you see the structure of the primary system at a glance. This use of space nicely dramatizes the politics of exclusion. Furthermore, if someone successfully gains church membership, the ability to change seats becomes a powerful moment of promotion, acceptance, and power.

Gamemasters

When the game begins, instructors cease being the center of attention. In order to empower the players, they often shift into what appears to be a more passive stance, but it is actually a more active and time-consuming method of instruction; it just is not as visible. Even so, confused players still look to the GM for guidance. This reinforces the need for simple and easily understandable rules and procedures. If players can grasp them independently, the GM can more safely fade into the background.

Regardless, players *still* look to the GM, so it is important to clarify the role of the GM at the outset. There are a number of overlapping possibilities, and in most cases, GMs will need to fill several of these functions at different points in the course of a game. Just give direction about when different functions are needed. Also include a caveat in the gamebook, which makes it clear that the GM can change the rules or the parameters of the game in midstream provided these changes advance the learning objectives of the game.

Umpire. Regardless of the care with which games are constructed, disputes arise between players. Anticipate likely disputes by addressing them in the gamebook. This allows players to police one another. Still, you cannot anticipate every odd combination of events. Players do inventive, weird, and unpredictable things. As Patrick Coby noted when describing the IM of his *Henry VIII and the Reformation Parliament*, "I tell instructors how to manage every foreseeable contingency. But not all contingencies have been foreseen."[12] When the unforeseen inevitably occurs, the GM must act as an umpire. In these cases, the best call is whatever advances the game towards its learning objectives. Once again, this suggests that a clear statement of those objectives probably aids in the operation of the game.

Facilitator. Customarily, GMs set up the game with several sessions of traditional instruction and end it with a debriefing and postmortem. During the game they work to help players who are struggling with the material or with the game. Sometimes, if everyone is confused, the GM needs to call a time out in order to clarify the situation.

Technician. Usually, GMs are the only people with full knowledge of the game mechanism. Thus, they must devote attention to managing it. If these duties peak at certain points in the game make sure that the GM has forewarning, and provide a checklist for running those parts of the game. If applicable, provide a "props list." In cases that involve a lot of variables, it can be a good idea for the GM to resolve the outcomes outside of the regular session. It is difficult to be a GM with a room full of highly emotional players looking over your shoulder as you attempt to puzzle out a complicated chart that requires multiple die rolls.

Arbiter. If a game is moving into distractingly ahistorical territory, it is the responsibility of the GM to move it back on to the path of historical plausibility. Ideally, rather than requiring overt intervention, this can be done with news reports that shift the situation on to more plausible ground between sessions.

---

[12] Patrick Coby, "Reacting to the Past: Faculty Lounge," Facebook Group, Nov. 16, 2011.

Reality check. Even if a game remains historically plausible, the GM should remind players that their actions have consequences. David Henderson notes, "When my Athens students vote to accept the Socratic's position that only the educated can vote, I always come in with quiz the next day to see who can actually vote."[13]

Special guest star. All of the functions of the GM described above are essential for any game. Players *need* umpires, facilitators, technicians, arbiters and a reality check. However, other functions are also possible. GMs may also step into the game sheathed in a historical persona. For example, in *Greenwich Village, 1913: Suffrage, Labor, and the New Woman* the GM may take on a temporary role as a reporter for the *New York Times*. This allows for some hard, abrasive questioning that might not otherwise take place. The GM assumes the role with the help of a prop – a hat with a "Press" tag in the brim – which signifies that something special is happening. When the reporter departs, the GM removes the hat and the role is dissolved. This helps make it clear to the players that the role is temporary. After whatever needs to happen has happened, GMs must be able to return to their other roles.

However, some players have difficulty accepting this reversion. That is why, even if you use notional props to make it clear when the GM steps into a role, you must be wary of asking your GMs to do this. If, while playing a role, the GM takes actions that dramatically change the course of the game, it can become too much like a piece of *deus ex machina*. In these cases, disadvantaged players may accuse the GM of rigging the game against them.

Furthermore, as David Henderson notes, "If the Gamemaster becomes part of the game, then the instructor is back in charge in ways that I think subvert the whole idea of empowering the

---

[13] David Henderson, "Reacting to the Past: Faculty Forum," Facebook Group, Nov. 8, 2011.

students to run the show."[14] Consequently, the default role of the GM should always be "instructor."

The Gamebook

Altering the classroom space and the functioning of the instructor are obvious and dramatic changes, which every player can see. The third element of the game is the context and that is relayed through the gamebook.

RTTP designs customarily devote several sessions to traditional instruction before play begins. These draw heavily upon the gamebook. They usually include discussion of the historical context, a brief walk through the salient issues, an explanation of the game mechanism, and the distribution of role sheets. They may also include opportunities for players to interact informally and in role.

Encourage players to begin engaging the intellectual collisions by breaking down the key positions and disagreements throughout the game materials. Address them in the vignette, contextualize them in the historical essay, chart out procedures for debating them with the rules, impose structure on these discussions with the schedule, and transform them into personal or group objectives with the role sheets.

The first piece of reading most players complete is the vignette. These are brief pieces of historical fiction. Their most important function is to begin immersing players into the milieu of the game. To this end, many designers write vignettes from a first or second person point of view. Often these are cinematic "walking tours" of the venue for the game, which allow the players to become briefly acquainted with the main issues, personalities, and ideas. Players generally read it before discussing the content or

---

[14] David Henderson, "Reacting to the Past: Faculty Forum," Facebook Group, Nov. 7, 2011.

structure of the game and before they read their role sheets. Consequently, it must be *very* accessible and short.

The essential historical background for the game should be provided in an essay that is textbook-like in tone and quality. As the game progresses, it should serve as a reference tool for the players, so it should be clearly organized with section titles. In early stages of game development, designers often use a chapter or two of a scholarly secondary source as a stand-in for this essay, and this often initially works well, but as the game develops, and the needs of the players become clearer, writing an original, purpose-built piece becomes desirable. These essays do not usually require original primary source research; instead they digest recent work on the topic into an undergraduate-friendly essay.

The shortest, and perhaps most thoroughly consulted, part of the gamebook contains the rules. RTTP games have two sorts of rules. The *explicit rules* are the ones that actually get written down. They describe and give order to player interactions with the game mechanism and one another. Consequently, they should focus on explaining the sort of choices that players will confront and how they should take appropriate action in terms of the game mechanism. Since you want players focused on the experience of the game rather than making sense of the rules, keep this section brief. In most cases, explicit rules make up the shortest part of the gamebook. It may only be a few pages long.

These rules only model a few aspects of a rich and complex historical situation. Many more "rules" exist in the historical events that form a dense background to the game. The existence of this vast array of *implicit rules* facilitates the brevity of this section.

Players generally understand these limits, and respect them as part of playing the game. When they attempt to push beyond them, it is usually due to anachronistic thinking rather than a misreading of the context.

The relationship between explicit and implicit rules can be fluid. You may want to encourage inventive players to mine this wealth of information for inspiration and, potentially, the creation of new explicit rules. Even if you do not encourage them, some players will attempt to mine the historical record in order to gain an advantage over their peers. When they complete this research, they usually request some sort of special power from the GM.

Provide the GM with guidance about what to do when this happens. The first consideration you should address is the question of new rules in general. Should GMs even contemplate them? If your game mechanism is very finely tuned, perhaps not, yet you should probably err on the side of permissiveness. Besides encouraging independent research, provisions for inventing new rules can help your game develop. Some of the explicit rules that now appear in published games began as efforts by striving players to gain advantage.

However, one danger of allowing new rules is that other players will see them as "cheats." Consequently, if your game allows new rules, consider following these guidelines:

- Wait at least one session before activating a new rule
- Require the inventive players to provide historical documentation
- Also require a rationale that the new rule will "make the game better" rather than simply providing tactical advantage

GMs should remind players that new rules may operate in the ways in which the proposers hoped. In fact, they may backfire. In addition, these rules may not operate in secrecy. Their existence must be announced to all of the players.[15]

---

[15] Jeff Hyson on the "Eunuchs?" thread of the RTTP China Forum, accessed Nov. 10, 2009.

Complexity

In describing how he designs simulations, Clark Aldrich describes the delicate balance of deciding how much information to impart:

> If you present *too little* information to the end-learner, the person can become lost and frustrated. The user would turn on the simulation, have no idea what was going on, flail about, do badly (or worse, do well!), and end the experience with a negative feeling. If you present *too much* guiding information, the simulation becomes linear content … The player then is just following instructions, never bringing in his or her own judgment of skills.[16]

Finding this balance can be tough, and it usually emerges as a result of playtesting, but you can take steps toward achieving this with your design.

First, make your game mechanism and the rules that govern it as simple as possible. As Tracy Fullerton reminds us, "The less well that players understand your rules, whether rationally or intuitively, the less likely they will be able to make meaningful choices within the system and the less sense they will have of being in control of the gameplay."[17] Unlike most historical writing, which encourages the treatment of wide ranges of actors and ideas, game designs need to be limited in scope. The easiest way to deal with this problem is to have very few rules, focused on certain problems in a specific venue at a set time. The more manageable the rule set, the more quickly and fully players engage the game.

Consequently, you must simplify historical processes a great deal. This can give designers fits because of their commitment to historical accuracy, but sacrifices are necessary if your game is

---

[16] Clark Aldrich, *Simulations and the Future of Learning* (San Francisco: Pfeiffer, 2004), 59-60.
[17] Fullerton, 71.

going to work as a *game*. (Disclosing your simplifications in the gamebook can help salve these pains).

All this is more easily said than done. Dunnigan notes that "It is very difficult to keep a game design project simple. Once you get going there are tremendous temptations to add this and add that."[18] Recognize that each additional element you add to the game mechanism makes the game *exponentially* more difficult to grasp. The first few additions are easy, but the comprehension curve is steep.

Simplicity facilitates ease of play and understanding, but a mechanism that seems simple to you may remain opaque to some players and GMs. Consequently, provide multiple chances to understand the rules. Explain the elements of your game mechanism repeatedly, and pay particular attention to the functioning of the primary system. In addition to providing an overview of its operations in the gamebook, use role sheets to let players know how and when they should plan on engaging the game mechanism.

Even so, some players will not master the rules until the game is well underway. As game designer Steve Semler points out, "Often, a game can make a concept easier to understand by embedding the concept into the rules and play of the game. As people play the game, they can grasp the idea of how the concept actually works."[19]

As much as you strive for simplicity complexity simply may be unavoidable. If this is the case, there are some things you can do to ease players into an understanding of your game mechanism as they play the game.

---

[18] Dunnigan.

[19] Steve Semler, "Games vs. Simulations," April 2001, www.learningsim.com/content/lsnews/games_sims.html

Quizzes. In order to make sure players familiarize themselves with the key elements of the historical context and functioning of the game mechanism, consider including some reading comprehension quizzes, which can be completed at the instructor's discretion. For the most part, these are straightforward multiple choice quizzes. In addition to encouraging close reading of game materials, quizzes can provide an opportunity for team-building. If they are completed in groups they can begin melding those players together into factions. An added (or alternative) incentive for strong performance on quizzes can appear in the form in-game advantages for high scorers.

Speeches. If your game mechanism is especially complex, assign some roles speech topics that explain the functioning of the system early in the game.

Player officials. Assign some roles the responsibility to maintain different aspects of the game mechanism.

Specialization. Do not ask players to master *every* aspect of the game mechanism. Instead, make sure everyone interacts with the primary system and then focus individuals on particular secondary systems.

Sequence. Reveal the different elements of the game mechanism in stages. Introducing the rules incrementally prevents players from becoming overwhelmed. In addition, it can provide opportunities to shake things up during the middle of the game. If you use this approach, simplify the operation of the game mechanism for the opening session(s) and inform players that the complexity will increase as the game proceeds. Otherwise, when the GM introduces a new element, players will complain that the game is being rigged against them or, worse yet, that the GM has become an adversary.[20]

Schedule

It is tempting to let players explore the issues for themselves, but (particularly at the outset of the game), they need some guidance. This is provided by your schedule. The trick is to provide enough structure to focus debate without making the game seem like a reenactment. The latter will leave players – particularly those with roles that historically "lost" the conflicts that appear in the game – with a sense that the game is rigged against them. Generally, a sequence of events provides a happy medium between a rigid structure and chaos.

Patriots, Loyalists & Revolution in New York City treads this path well. In order to advance towards their ultimate objectives, role sheets compel some players to get certain issues resolved promptly. This encourages them to push the discussion along toward some sort of action using both primary and secondary systems. Once certain decisions are made by the players, the GM introduces new issues and/or complications to old issues. The combination of these player-generated outcomes and the outside events that are introduced by the GM move the game along at a good clip without requiring a rigid schedule. The debate never becomes stale; while the issues shift, they never do so dramatically enough to make the players feel cheated. Their actions still have consequences. Decisions they made in the early sessions help shape the situations they confront as the game proceeds.

To prevent players from becoming disoriented as the situation changes, they should be able to anticipate some of what is coming in the next one or two sessions, but they do not need to see where the game will ultimately end up. Indeed, if they do, many players

---

[20] Greenblat, 63.

start developing endgame strategies, which may disengage them from the cut and thrust of the sessions preceding the end of the game. For example, the gamebook for *Kentucky, 1861: A Nation in the Balance* only describes the discussion topics for the first two sessions of the game. The topics for subsequent days are delivered by the GM as the game unfolds. One drawback of this approach is that it can be difficult for players to prepare good speeches on short notice. However, once the game is in motion, players will grasp their core ideology well enough to adapt to the situation as it develops.

Even if concealing details about the future from the players makes for good game play, the shape of things to come must not be hidden from the GM. The IM must provide a full schedule that clearly describes the sequence(s) that the game should take. Any options for the timing must be made very clear so that the GM can review them in order to see the trajectory of the game as a whole.

Therefore, an outline schedule for the entire game, including the introductory and debriefing sessions, should appear in the gamebook. If possible, avoid setting rigid or specific requirements for a specific number of sessions. Do not force GMs to retrofit your game to fit the requirements of their institutions. Give them a variety of schedules so they can use the game with ease.
Build in a measure of flexibility so GMs may tailor the game to fit their particular circumstances.

Counterfactuals

It may be necessary to manipulate certain historical elements in order to improve the functioning of your game. The most common counterfactual element is bringing historical figures who never met into conversation together. For example, *Greenwich Village* brings a host of bohemians together for a series of regular meetings in a café. These people were never all assembled at the same venue for a series of discussions, but the counterfactual works because they inhabited the same milieu and were familiar with one another's ideas.

Other games speed up the clock on certain historical developments. The *Confucianism* game features some scholars that are members of the Eastern Grove movement. Historical records first mention the group several years after the setting of the game, but the counterfactual works because it is plausible that the foundations of the movement were being laid at the time during which the game is set.

These alterations follow the guidelines for counterfactuals cogently laid out by game designer John Moser. He accepts them as long as they:

- Improve game play
- Are plausible
- Are clearly identified in the game book

Both of the counterfactuals described above fit these criteria. Without a venue and regular interactions, the *Greenwich Village* game would not work. In the *Confucianism* game, one faction needs additional leadership, which the members of the Eastern Grove can provide. The fixes are plausible, so they are acceptable.

The last point is easy to overlook or elide, so be particularly conscientious; make sure to fully describe and justify any counterfactuals. Do not list them in the IM with the expectation that the instructor will cover them in the debriefing. Keep them up front. Full disclosure decreases the chances that some players will develop an inaccurate understanding of the past.

In order to make sure you have all of the elements you need in your gamebook, please consult the following template. The text for the section on "How to React" is boilerplate shared by all of the games in the series.

Front Matter
    Title Page
    Map
    Table of Contents
Historical Setting
    Vignette
    Historical context and background
The Game Itself
    How to React
    Major issues for debate
    Rules and procedures
    Structure
    Roles and factions
    Counterfactuals
Core Texts
Supplemental documents
Appendices
Selected bibliography
Acknowledgements

4. The Roles

In order to plunge into the game, players need questions answered about where they stand in relation to the game mechanism and one another. The different materials in the gamebook provide some answers, but the most important documents for most players are their roles sheets. They are their little lifeboats on a tempestuous sea.

Some games, especially while in development, rely on sketchy roles. This may present opportunities for players to determine their own positions on different issues, which is empowering, but without significant research, players inadvertently take stands that are anachronistic or implausible. They also may not understand how they should relate to other players. Thus, if at all possible, ensure that your roles are as well developed as is possible. Even if it encourages innovation and imaginative thinking, no one wants a leaky lifeboat. Even worse is the lifeboat that needs to be constructed while you are busy trying to tread water.

Often, RTTP creates bewilderment because players know little about the subject of the game. The gamebook and setup days go a long way to addressing this, but they cannot fully allay the anxiety felt by many players, much of which stems from the differences between conventional classroom experiences and RTTP. Increased levels of active participation, accountability, and peer interaction can be intimidating, so students accustomed to passive learning often become uncomfortable. They are reluctant to participate because, lacking high levels of expertise, they fear being wrong. In addition, many find it disconcerting when the other players (who are similarly ill-informed), rather than the instructor (a certified expert), become their interlocutors. Also: they are all saying different and sometimes contradictory things – sometimes all at once. *Who has the correct answer? Will this be on the test?*

The most important instrument for reducing this fear and confusion is the role sheet. Players cling to it for safety and reassurance. The information it provides is essential to begin functioning in the game. Unlike the gamebook, which is (theoretically) read by everyone, each role sheet is read by a handful of players at most. If it is a unique role, it only gets read by a single player. This may tempt you to focus your efforts on the game materials that everyone will read. *Do not fall prey to this temptation!* Role sheets are the most important elements of any RTTP game. Without them, players are lost.

Involuntary play

RTTP also creates confusion because people generally consider playing games to be a voluntary activity. One may choose to *play cards* or *play tag* without an obvious institutional compulsion to do so. RTTP is different. In order to complete the course you *must* play the game. The only way to opt out of the game is to not take the class. Since participation is mandatory rather than voluntary, RTTP games might be more properly labeled *simulations*, *matches* or *exercises*, but games they are.

Perhaps the RTTP experience is best compared to involvement in team sports. Participants "play Reacting" in the same way one might "play football" after joining a football team. By enrolling in the course you opt to become part of the team. Therefore you have agreed to participate in the team's *practices* (the opening days of the game) and *scrimmages* (the days when the game is actually running). To draw the metaphor out fully, the instructor becomes both *coach* and *referee*.

However, regardless of how you conceptualize it, not every player specifically opted into the game experience. Consequently, while many other concepts that we generally associate with "play" are present, every designer must remember that for some players participation is, to some degree, involuntary. Every instructor and institution deals with this in a particular way, and while deep consideration of every possible approach to this situation is beyond your responsibilities as a designer, you should keep this issue in mind because it means your game will be played by people with a wide variety of motivations and levels of engagement.

Consequently, when you are designing your roles, try to accommodate a variety of personalities, motivations, and abilities. Remember: not everyone is a flamboyant extrovert who loves to read. As game designer Mary Jane Treacy puts it,

> There have to be roles for the introverted and shy, the quiet intellectual, the abrasive aggressive, the calculating, the snooty aloof, the wildly insecure, etc. ... Weak students, those who do not want to give the time to the game, and resistant students need to be brought into the world of the game via roles that can be managed with minimal effort, but could be expanded if the student were to catch fire.[21]

Some games (notably Treacy's *Greenwich Village*) include "casting" questions as part of a pre-game quiz. This can be particularly important for roles that require deceit, alienation, or lots of work. At the very least, include tips about casting in the IM. If certain roles work best with certain personalities, let the GM know.

---

[21] Email from Mary Jane Treacy, July 4, 2011.

Reading the gamebook and participating in the opening sessions set the stage, while the role sheets set individual terms for beginning to play, but the game remains inert until the game mechanism begins to draw players into meaningful interactions with one another. Consequently, you must compel players to enter the game – even before they fully understand what they are doing.

What must I do?

The more explicitly role sheets describe the duties and obligations associated with each role, the less anxiety players experience. The degree of explicitness about assignments in the role sheet is usually inversely proportional to the level of anxiety at the beginning of the game. Remember: it's a lifeboat. Before learning anything else, you must know how to prevent yourself from sinking. If you have never needed one before, clear instructions are always welcome.

Initiating the interaction between players and the game mechanism is an essential first step towards meaningful play. Most players enter a game in the company of strangers. Even if they know one another, they do not know how to talk with one another about the ideas they will need to express in the game. The game is the matrix through which they must interact. It makes their conversations meaningful. Thus, they need to relate to the game before they begin to understand how they relate to one another.

Since players must take action in order to enter the game, they must be compelled to take action even if they do not want to. If players only act when they feel like it or when the GM goads them, the game ceases to function as a game. It becomes something more like a traditional class discussion.

Consequently, every role must include a *compulsion* to interact with the primary system of the game mechanism during the *first* game session. The easiest way to do this is to require all players to vote on something. This is a minor step, but it is an important one. When a vote is informed by their role rather than their own, personal opinions, they have begun playing the game.

It is important for players to eventually understand why they vote in certain ways, but at the outset of the game it is more important for them to begin playing than it is for them to explain the rationale behind their votes or to understand exactly what is going on. For example, if you are learning how to play tag, the instruction "don't get tagged" is all you need to know. Once you are running around, the other elements of the game – dodging, getting frozen, becoming *IT*, etc. – become easy to learn. The sooner your players start "running around" the better; help your players interact with the primary system early and often.

Who am I?

The game creates a potentially liminal space where players may become something other than what they are; roles provide guidance about what that "something else" might be; so role sheets must provide players with several things. Foremost among them is a place within the game. Players need to understand how they fit into the big picture both intellectually and functionally. To facilitate this, they need to know where they stand in relation to the *intellectual collisions*, the *game mechanism*, and *other players*.

What do I think?

In order to foreground intellectual collisions at the outset, it is a good idea to provide roles with specific textual references to support their positions. In addition to providing intellectual grounding, this helps ensure that players incorporate the documents that accompany the game into their arguments. Without these cues, some players fall back on arguing from ahistorical, present-day convictions.

Once the game is in motion, many players become deeply engaged, but their engagement is often with the most political aspects of the game – forming alliances, trading favors, building coalitions, and stabbing one another in the back. These may all be important factors in the game, but it is essential to keep intellectual collisions front and center. This heightens the need to ground the roles in particular documents. Draw players back to the readings that lie at the intellectual core of the game by making this an essential element of achieving victory over the course of the game. There are several ways to do this. At the least, direct players to re-read specific sections of the assigned documents when confronting certain issues.

More mechanical ways of encouraging document use may be tied to the completion of various assignments. For example, some games require players to reference certain documents or ideas in their writing assignments and/or formal speeches. Others are stricter. They require players to reference a specific number of documents in their writing assignments and/or formal speeches.

Supplemental documents can be useful in rounding out the historical context. This is particularly useful for games that are built around central texts since roles that are posed in opposition to the ideas promoted by a central text need some intellectual ammunition. If these roles lack resources, they can suffer an intellectual collapse. However, unless these documents are tied to specific roles, they often go unread and unused by all but the keenest players. Consequently, if you include a document in the gamebook, guide several roles to it via their role sheets. If only one or two players really need it, append it to their role sheets.

Players understand the ideas of the game through the lenses of their roles, so they should have a biography to draw upon. They need to understand where they are coming from, so help them grasp their past relations with the central ideas, the game mechanism, and other players. If they know these things, they are better situated to engage in the game. Still, as is the case with explicit rules, you cannot provide information about everything.

Gaps will always exist, and players may need to fill them. When this appears likely, provide explicit instructions that the player should create historically appropriate details before the game begins. For example, in *Anne Hutchinson* members of the church are curious about the family and community background of people applying for membership. They latter group should be able to anticipate this interest so they can develop these aspects of their roles before other players start questioning them.

Players with roles that are not modeled on specific historical figures should have the opportunity to select "game names." This has several benefits. First, it allows players to begin to take ownership over their roles. Second, it creates distance between the player's identity as a person and the player's identity as a role. This may be particularly important in games that require players to relate ideas – racist, sexist, etc. – that are particularly at odds with contemporary society.

In order to get a wide array of ideas and points of view into the mix, define the extremes of the ideological spectra for your planned intellectual collisions. In order to facilitate discussion, you may need to over-populate extremist positions. This helps ensure that the intellectual collisions actually occur. However, if you overburden the extremes and only have a few moderates, it can throw off the balance of your game. If reconciliation and compromise appear impossible, some players will shut down because they cannot perceive the possibility of a win; others will turn their thoughts to violence.

What can I do?

Players need to be able to initiate a variety of possible actions, and in order to understand their options, players need information. Without it they will be paralyzed or they will behave erratically.[22]

The first concern of most players is developing an understanding how they fit into the game mechanism. There are several reasons of this. First and foremost among these is because they are concerned about how they will be assessed by the GM. If they do not understand how to interact with the game, they will not be able to do well, and then, they reason, they will receive poor marks from the GM's instructor aspect.

Use the gamebook to explain how roles fit into the game mechanism by describing the resources that each controls (e.g., influence, votes, land, money, troops, etc.), and by offering advice on how to use them. If a particular role controls a disproportionate amount of any resource, make this clear to everyone. In *Constantine and the Council of Nicaea,* Emperor Constantine is clearly not "just another role." Consequently, his power and influence must be made clear to everyone even while his motives and weaknesses may remain concealed.

Some games are set in times of chaos so it is not entirely clear what powers are associated with certain roles. In *Rousseau, Burke, and Revolution in France, 1791,* the *actual* powers of King Louis XVI differ considerably from the powers ascribed to him by tradition. If a new constitution is created, those powers will likely shift again, and they may not be congruent with the powers described in the constitution. This can be very confusing, but in general, players accept uncertainty as long as it is clearly a part of the game rather than a lapse in their understanding of the situation

---

[22] Much of this rubric is modeled on "Anatomy of a choice" from Salen and Zimmerman, 64.

or a flaw in the game materials. Anything about a role that is confusing should be purposefully so.

Similarly, players accept the existence of secret powers. Players love having secret powers, and even if they do not have them, they like knowing they are out there. However if a secret power is employed against them, they may become resentful. Consequently, secret powers should generally dispense blessings rather than curses. They should also tend to come into play toward the end of the game.

Embedding charts in role sheets can be good way to convey detailed information about possible actions. For example, a handful of the roles in *Defining a Nation: India on the Eve of Independence, 1945,* include detailed charts describing the possible results of the Communist player's attempts to foment rebellion. This information is very important for these roles, but others need not be burdened by the details even though they may care very much about the results. Some players appreciate having all of this information available so that they can weigh their options, but others become daunted by their complexity. So, unless there is a special and extenuating circumstance, it is best to describe objectives in prose; leave the charts to the IM.

What do other people think about me?

Explaining the relationships between roles allows players to more fully inhabit them. As an introduction to the relationships, the gamebook should include a *dramatis personae* section that sketches out the important public information about all of the roles. Use this section to provide information about ideological positions, control of resources, and particularly important or intense relationships between roles. Make public as much information as possible, but use role sheets to provide any private information about relationships between various roles. There may be secrets.

It is useful to include lists of friends and enemies on role sheets, but make it clear that everyone does not fall into one of these categories. The lists of friends and allies are particularly important because they help to ameliorate the degree to which players are confused and intimidated by the uncertainty of the game.

Factions provide this sort of support in the clearest form, and players who are members of factions benefit from the support of their peers. They become a team.

Indeterminates present more of a challenge because it is difficult to group them together into likeminded groups without turning them into new factions. Consequently, it is probably a good idea to take special care to provide some comfort in their role sheets. Reassure them that they have great power. If possible, direct them towards a few roles that are likely to become future allies. Finally, as Joan Sitomer put it, let them know that "Students don't want other students to lose. They do want to do better than their opponents, but they still really support one another."[23]

Although zealots can be intellectually straight-forward, they are often difficult roles to play because their inflexible, dogmatic outspokenness often leads other players to shun them. Moderates can be challenging because you start to feel like you are the only sane person in the room. Since games are usually set in moments of dramatic change, players with conservative roles may feel as if everyone (including history) is against them. Consequently, it may be useful to clump roles together into factions. The strongest relationships between roles exist when they are gathered into factions, which are important structural elements of many RTTP games. These provide players with like-minded allies, which allows for bonding, cooperation, and teamwork.

---

[23] Personal conversation with Joan Sitomer. March 24, 2013.

Making the identity and objectives of faction members identical facilitates strong bonds of trust and cooperation. This can be particularly useful for inexperienced players – it eases them into the pedagogy with a peer group. Requiring joint assignments can help to cement these relationships. For example, in *Revolution in France,* factions must work together to compile, edit, and publish newspapers.

Creating variations in identity and objectives among faction members weakens these bonds, but it allows a more complicated dynamic within factions, additional ideas (often with shadings of meaning), and a more accurate modeling of complex historical situations.

Indeterminate roles ensure that your game becomes something other than a debate or yelling match. They are an in-game audience, which is open to persuasion. This is a critical ingredient because without the opportunity to actually convince someone to adopt their position, players may become disengaged.

These players possess the ability to determine the outcome of the game, so they possess an enormous amount of power, but these roles can be emotionally demanding; being an indeterminate can be awfully lonely. Consequently, indeterminate role sheets should boost the morale of their players by assuring them that they are very, very important. In addition, instruct other players to lobby indeterminates. Finally, use the IM to encourage GMs to touch base with the indeterminates.

Particularly pivotal or put-upon indeterminates should be cloned. The presence of a buddy ensures the vitality of the position. At early stages, *Forest Diplomacy* featured a single Iroquois representative, but in playtesting, this player always felt ostracized and overwhelmed. Sometimes this feeling became so intense that the player withdrew from the action. This passivity removed an important element of the game. Creating a mini-faction by cloning the role strengthened the determination and raised the morale of the Iroquois players even though nothing about the role changed vis-à-vis the game mechanism.

Since players with indeterminate roles may easily become passive, structure their roles so that they must secure the assistance of others in order to fulfill their objectives. This is a good way to use secondary systems. If some players need something from other players, they are compelled to talk to them.

If this seems too structured or coercive, then use indeterminate role sheets to suggest possible alliances. If these players lack such cues, they often simply wait to be approached. This may be important to the dynamic for particular roles, but most of the time, you want to encourage them to interact with other players.

If you have a large number of indeterminate roles, you may even want to develop a sort of "matchmaker" role to get them to talk with one another. *Greenwich Village* features socialite Mabel Dodge. Part of her function in the game is to encourage indeterminates to collaborate with one another.

Instead of fully indeterminate roles, many games include a degree of indeterminacy in *every* role. This requires significantly more work to ensure balance, and it can make games more complex, but it can result in a game with a higher degree of historical accuracy as well as adding more intrigue and need for negotiation. Whatever course you pursue, in terms of game mechanics, the important thing is to make sure that there are roles open to persuasion on every issue that is central to the game.

Indeterminates should not be fully indeterminate. Indeed, if they are, they become rather difficult to play. When you can be persuaded to adopt *any* position on *any* issue, it is difficult to get much intellectual traction. Consequently indeterminates need some sort of an intellectual anchor. Give your indeterminates intellectual heft and provide them with documents to support their positions.

Indeterminates need not be moderates. If you want an idea that falls outside of the central intellectual collisions to be a part of the game, associate it with an indeterminate role. This player then becomes an advocate for that idea. Tying a supplementary text to such a role can give a peripheral idea a place in an already full game without requiring everyone to read about it in depth. Once players with these roles can understand and articulate their position on the single issue that is central to their role, they are free to interpret the other issues in the game through this lens. For example, in the *Athens* game the Bearded Artisan is tasked with bringing gender issues to the Assembly, but the player is free to be persuaded on the other issues.

Other times, individual indeterminate roles are "wreckers." In other words, they hold positions so far outside that of the majority of players that they may try to get the central negotiations of the game to collapse. In *Defining a Nation* the leader of the Communist Party seeks something that no other role does: an uprising of the working class; discord between the other players increases the chances of Communist success in India. This can be a great way to complicate a situation, but if you include a wrecker, you must also provide an "off switch" in case the player becomes so disruptive that it distracts everyone from the core intellectual collisions. In this case, the Governor General of India can send the Communist to jail.

Not every GM wants tangential issues to become central, but in the hands of a determined player, a peripheral role can take over the game. Consequently, it is important to provide guidance in the IM about the ideas and situations that different tangential roles might introduce. Ideally, the structure of your game should allow GMs to tailor the game to meet their particular needs and learning objectives.

Many games include roles that are composites of several historical figures rather than actual individuals. In terms of game design, this approach has much to recommend it. The chief benefit is that it allows the designer to fit roles more neatly into the game mechanism. The primary downside is that players often become more engaged when playing roles that are modeled upon specific historical figures. They like playing real people and often carefully research them. Consequently, exhaust reality before turning to invention. Often, the idiosyncrasies of historical figures humanize roles that if structured as composites become simplistic expressions of particular ideologies.

This problem becomes more intense when the historical figure is some sort of "celebrity." Players often have difficulty separating the historical actuality of the figure from their preconceptions. In addition, some players may become uncomfortable playing the role of a figure they greatly admire (or detest). Imagine the difficulty most players would have with Jesus or Hitler.

Several games deal with this by removing central figures from the mix. For example, *Defining a Nation* separates Gandhi into two roles of Gandhi supporters, and the *Athens* game keeps Socrates off stage even though he is on trial for part of the game. His ideas are represented by the members of the Socratic faction.

Other games, like *Anne Hutchinson* and *Charles Darwin, the Copley Medal and the Rise of Naturalism, 1861-64,* use the "friend of" approach, which drops the specificity of celebrity identity while retaining the essential ideology of specific historical figures.

Both approaches have advantages, but they often result in player confusion. The Radical Democrat faction pointedly asks, "Where is Socrates anyway? He must answer for his crimes!" Since games featuring figures like Emperor Constantine, George Washington, and Joseph Stalin seem to work just fine, whenever possible, I recommend bringing celebrities into the game as roles. Just use the IM to make it clear to the GM that these roles are special and may require casting and write the role sheets with care.

How do I win?

The hope of achieving victory animates many players.[24] *Don't fight this!* Help players find motivation within the liminal world of the game by providing them with plenty of clear, achievable objectives. Just make sure they pass through your intellectual collisions on their way to victory.

Players usually try to achieve some sort of compromise. Most players do not want anyone to lose. For some games this is not a problem, but for others, it is. Consequently, you must take active steps to prevent historically implausible compromise from developing. If a hard-won compromise is your desired outcome, complicate the situation so that it cannot happen quickly or easily.

Some designers prefer vague objectives because they allow players to discover roles on their own terms, but this often leads to confusion, disconnection, and/or implausible compromises. They also usually culminate in debriefings in which all the players claim victory because they poorly understood what was being asked of them.

Clearly structuring objectives allows players to move more quickly into debating the merits of various ideas rather than spending a great deal of time figuring out the particulars of how to achieve victory. Use the gamebook, role sheets, and IM to explain how players can translate their desire to fulfill objectives into action.

The problems players need to contend with must be laid out with some immediacy. Otherwise, players enter the game lackadaisically. Fuel their desire to win by raising the stakes of the game for their roles. Make it clear that the outcome of player actions matter. If they fail to achieve their objectives, the results should be dire. *Your death with be horrible and lingering! Your people will be wiped from the face of the earth!* Conversely, if they

---

[24] Greenblat, 63.

achieve their objectives, the results should be impressive and possibly ahistorical. *All hail Emperor Mark Antony!*

Most roles include multiple objectives. Sometimes these are equally weighted, but it can be advantageous (and historically accurate) for some roles to prioritize some objectives above others. There seem to be four main ways to deal with this.

An easy but flawed approach is to weight objectives mathematically. This method is easy for players and GMs to understand, but it potentially creates some problems because players gravitate towards the math.

When I attended my second RTTP conference to play the *Athens* game, I almost walked away from the entire pedagogy after a well-meaning student-preceptor put his hand on top of my dog-eared copy of *The Republic*. "Don't worry about that," he said, gently pushing it down to the tabletop. His other hand framed page 31 of the gamebook, which assigns numerical values to various possible outcomes of the game. "Worry about this."

This is typical player behavior, so you should avoid describing objectives in numerical terms. If you give them numbers to juggle, players focus on the math instead of on the ideas; the game becomes an exercise in number-crunching. Additional problems arise when players broker historically implausible but mathematically sound compromises.[25]

Another approach, which has less potential for distorting player behavior, is to place objectives in two tiers. In addition to "regular" objectives, include descriptions of what needs to be done in order to achieve a *big win*. Similarly, explain what a *total loss* looks like. The former should be quite difficult to achieve, but if the conditions can be met it results in a victory so complete, that the lesser objectives become unimportant.

---

[25] Koster, 118.

When used together, the *big win* and *total loss* define the boundaries of the spectrum of possibilities presented by the game. In most cases, players focus on their "regular" objectives, but the possibility of a *big win* or a *total loss* still shapes their behavior. They help define the intellectual parameters of their roles and develop a sense about what can be reasonably sacrificed.

Another, more subjective, way to deal with prioritizing objectives is to have players assert the degree to which they have achieved victory with a post-game writing assignment. This is particularly useful when players have a lot of idiosyncratic, role-specific objectives.

Such an assignment could, for example, explain the degree to which the achievement of certain objectives resulted in what the wargaming world would label as *decisive* victories as opposed to *tactical* victories. Similarly, players can try to argue their way out of defeat.

As an additional learning objective, such an assignment could be a good starting point for analyzing what historians have to say about the outcomes of the events modeled by the game. Are "victory" and "defeat" things that can be empirically defined or are they defined through discourse? In a wargame, it may be the former, but when considering the topics covered by RTTP games, the latter seems more appropriate.[26]

The final and easiest to manage approach is to simply provide the players with a ratio. For example, a role with five objectives might be required to fulfill four of them. This way, players gain some flexibility, but they remain focused on the ways in which other players respond to the give and take of the intellectual collisions. If the discussion seems to be turning against one of the outcomes they desire, they can decide to make a sacrifice. Similarly, if a strong majority is pushing in a direction that they

---

[26] Thanks to Natasha Gill for sparking my thinking on this matter.

favor, they can be confident that they have at least one objective sewn up.

Players can become overwhelmed when they first confront a list of victory objectives. Breaking large issues into smaller components that build upon one another allows players to grapple with complex ideas in a series of manageable debates. Rather than needing to contend with the entire scope of a large, unfamiliar, and complex issue all at once, their objectives order it into a sequence of smaller, interrelated components. As they tackle each component, their understanding of the whole increases. As the game advances this allows for culminating debates that deal with the issue as a whole. By the time these arrive, players are intellectually prepared to contend with them.

Additionally, slowing players down and forcing them to debate the merits of dramatic, epochal action prevents them from rushing into it. One good way to achieve this is to divide debate between separate sessions. For example, in *Japan, the West, and the Road to World War,* the Japanese government must pass a resolution to make preparations for military operations at least one session before it can actually launch an attack. Stair-stepping objectives in this fashion helps restrain especially passionate players who want to take dramatic actions without much discussion.

When objectives are parsed into steps, players need to have a good sense about how the results of their actions potentially affect future choices. Ideally, game materials make this clear, but given the variety of possible player actions, this information may need to come directly from the GM.

You may be concerned that this much structure will result in an overly scripted game. Don't fret. Even if you impose the order in which objectives must be met, players find all sorts of ways to subvert the order (through both action and inaction). Furthermore, as long as you provide them with sufficient room and rich ideas, the ways in which they make, support, and resolve their arguments in pursuit of those objectives will be myriad.

As they strive for victory, many players come to see various elements of the game as unfair. Usually, such complaints arise from players who have become heavily emotionally invested or from those who do not fully understand the game or their place within it. Usually, this accusation is nonsense, but sometimes it is a valid observation. In some games, the deck is stacked.

Tracy Lightcap sees the presence of power disparity as a positive because it makes the situations modeled by the games more realistic. He writes, "The most realistic aspect of Reacting games is that power is unevenly distributed and exercised by elites. ... Indeed, the energy in the games is largely due to the rising tensions between those in power and those who are sidelined."[27]

As he suggests, this creates is a tricky balance, which is best addressed through the composition of objectives. Those with a smaller measure of power will generally accept the situation as long as some sort of victory is possible. Even if victory is very hard to achieve, most players will dig in and persevere, but only as long as there is a shred of hope. In these cases, role sheets must be particularly attentive to the morale of players with little power.

In order to keep hope alive, structure the game so that important objectives cannot be achieved until the final session. This gives players long-term goal and it keeps them in the game.

If the resolution of a culminating issue is held off until the final session, even players who have been repeatedly defeated have good reason to stay engaged: they can win an amazing, come-from-behind victory. Similarly, players who have enjoyed a

---

[27] Tracy Lightcap, "Oppan Reacting Style! Creating Short Simulations Using Reacting to the Past," presented at the Georgia Political Science Association, Savannah, Georgia, Nov. 7, 2012.

series of victories must stay on their toes. If they become too complacent, they can still lose.

Psychologist Mihaly Csikszentmihalyi's concept of *flow* is often cited by game designers. He states that people are most happy when they are in a state of *flow*. (More colloquially, this is being *in the zone* or *in the groove*.) This state is entered when you become fully absorbed in an activity. Your concentration becomes so intense that the outside world falls away. You forget to eat and sleep because the activity becomes preeminent. Your brain chemistry may even change.

This is a particularly popular concept with electronic game designers because this sort of absorption is the *ne plus ultra* of a successful electronic game, but it is a feeling that should be familiar to almost everyone from musicians to athletes to artisans to researchers. The state is entered into when the challenge of a task is perfectly matched with one's skill. If the task is too easy, one becomes bored. If the task is too difficult, one becomes frustrated, but if skill and challenge are in equilibrium, *flow* results.[28]

Such a state is difficult to achieve in an RTTP game because there are so many players with various abilities making cognitive leaps at different times, but the concept is useful to keep in mind as you think about how to integrate players into the game. There must always be a challenge, but it must be calibrated to the ability of the players. Initially, the difficulty should be limited, but as the game progresses, challenges must be escalated in order to meet the players' growing familiarity with the game mechanism, the intellectual collisions, and one another.[29]

---

[28] Mihaly Csikszentmihalyi, *Flow: The Psychology of Optimal Experience* (New York: HarperCollins, 1991).
[29] Koster, 98.

Players respond positively to the challenges posed by RTTP, but they may become frustrated if they become confused. Importantly, almost everyone becomes confused at one point or another. In the survey I conducted in 2013, only 6% of players reported that they were never confused in the course of the game. The role sheet is the most important tool for confused players. 79% reported that it helped them when they became confused. The next most important resource was the GM with 71%. To help players and GMs as they struggle to process the game, end each role sheet with a short summary of objectives. This quick reference will help both players and GMs.

In order to make sure you have all of the elements you need in your role sheets, please consult the following template.

Name
Office & faction (if any)
Biography
Objectives/victory conditions
Responsibilities
- Duties
- Powers
- Assignments
Relationships
- With the big ideas
- With the texts
- With other people
Strategy advice
Selected sources
Briefly restated list of objectives
Special tokens (if any)
Role-specific readings (if any)

5. Playing the Game

Together, the written elements described above should convey the essence of the game. Polish them for clarity rather than comprehensiveness. Together, they form the gateway to the game; they are not the game itself. The game begins when players begin to *play*.

Games should move forward as a result of the internal logic of the game mechanism and schedule. It can be pleasant to watch a game cruising along, but the GM must remain attentive. Players must be tended and sometimes the game needs to be slowed or quickened.

Setting the stage

Even if rules do not call for it, many GMs find it useful to devote part of the first game session to a series of short introductory statements from all of the players so that everyone has a better basic sense of where people stand as the game begins. If your roles are particularly varied, it may be useful to incorporate this into the structure of your game. It also accustoms players to speaking in role. It can also be useful for players to have nametags or placards identifying them for the first few sessions of the game. Instead of burdening the GM with the job of making and distributing these, consider making it a responsibility attached to a certain role (or roles).

Opening the game with a peculiar event is a good way to signify the beginning of play. It draws the Magic Circle. Ideally, the responsibility to organize these events is scripted into certain roles. If some players are compelled to put these events into motion they often pull the others along. For example, the *Athens* game begins with a pig sacrifice. The gamebook makes it clear that the specifics of this ritual are unknown to history, which gives players the freedom to improvise without fear of "getting it right." The oddness and absurdity of this event helps to draw the circle. Similarly, *Kentucky, 1861,* begins with everyone taking an oath of office, which includes a promise to refrain from dueling. These help to convey the idea that the players have entered into another world in which their identities have shifted.

Initial debate

In order to ease players into the game, it is often useful to build the first game session around a predetermined debate on a single issue. This achieves several ends. It provides a procedural model for subsequent game sessions, sets events into motion, and invites players into the Magic Circle by:

- Requiring action on the part of many or all players.
- Revealing some allegiances.
- Modeling the functioning of the game mechanism.
- Dramatizing differences between the game world and the present.

After such an initial game session, players possess a more confident ownership of their roles and their place in the game. They begin to see how the game materials can come together. (Alternatively, they freak out because they have not yet done much of the reading.)

There are several ways to construct an initial debate, but most games begin with a specific problem.[30] For example, the *Athens* game begins with the issue of the Reconciliation Agreement. The question is: what shall democratic Athens do to mend itself after the ejection of the Thirty Tyrants?

In many ways, this initial session serves as a dry run through the game mechanism. Some players will not understand what is happening, but they may improve their understanding of the system through trial and error. Consequently, the initial issue should be either incidental to the rest of the game or the deck should be stacked so high that only one outcome is really possible. Otherwise, if a few players make some key procedural errors at the outset, it can sour the entire game.

Peter L. de Rosa, a history instructor, provides some good real-world advice about player comprehension of the game mechanism and the need for this sort of dry run. He found that the biggest problem using games in the classroom is rules comprehension. This is because many players,

> do not read the rules carefully if at all. They often treat this like any other assignment and do as little as possible. Others cannot make the necessary conceptual leaps on their own. ... Overall, about one-fourth learn the rules by reading them, another quarter after listening to explanations, a third group from attending the dry run, and the rest by playing the game.[31]

Voting at the conclusion of the initial debate can help deal with this problem in a number of ways. First, it allows players to see at

---

[30] Greenblat, 62.

[31] Peter L. de Rosa, "Wargames in Introductory History Courses," *Academic Gaming Review*, vol. 5, no. 2 (Spring 2003): http://www.gis.net/~pldr/wihc.html.

least part of the game mechanism in action. Second, it can push players away from present-mindedness. When, in the *Athens* game, free speech arguments are defeated by a gag rule on the citizens of Athens, it becomes abundantly clear that the world of the game is significantly different than the world inhabited by most players. Third, it is a good opportunity to see who has and has not understood the rules. In games with strong factions, players may subsequently provide some peer correction for players who misunderstood their roles or the game mechanism. In games without strong factions, the GM can communicate with inert players and those who took actions that were not in keeping with their roles. Together, these elements should prepare everyone for the second session when the game begins in earnest.

For all of its advantages, scripting the initial issue must be done carefully. If you are going to stack the deck, you must stack it high. Make sure that voting instructions on role sheets are very, very clear. In addition, make sure there are an abundance of voters in favor of the outcome you desire. All this is tricky because you must avoid making the outcome of the initial session *obviously* inevitable. This can make the losers feel cheated. In addition, it can make the winners sloppy. They may assume that everything is going to go their way. Consequently, even if the fix is in, it must be a real intellectual collision. Both sides of the debate must have good arguments, and the votes must come from the core of every role. The GM seems like a marionettist if players explain their votes by saying, "My role sheet says I need to vote this way."

One way to salve the frustration of those who lose an initial debate is to reward them for fighting the good fight. Consider adding some in-game advantage for those who argue their point particularly well. This can take away some of the sting and it can keep them fully engaged in the game. Alternatively, promise future revenge.

PIPs

"Personal Influence Points," or PIPs, are innovative approach that uses additional assignments to further immerse players in the world of the game first appeared in *Greenwich Village.* Throughout the game, players must earn PIPs by performing activities that relate to the game. Players might earn a few points for small gestures like wearing pro-IWW pins or they may go for bigger point counts by making art, staging rallies, or distributing information about contraception.

Players want to earn as many PIPs as possible for two reasons. First, it determines how many votes they may cast when the game reaches a climax in the final session. Thus, if they want their ideas to prevail, they and their supporters must accumulate a lot of points. Second, if they fail to accumulate a minimum number of points, they must write an additional essay.

This device achieves several ends. It engages players in the game, encourages collaboration, and – since some PIPs require the involvement of non-players – it breaks down the "fourth wall" by drawing people who are not in the game into the magic circle.

Cause and effect

Once players begin to interact with the game mechanism, they must be able to see the results. If players cannot see this relationship, they begin to doubt the meaningfulness of their actions.

The strength of this relationship depends on discernible feedback loops. As Salen and Zimmerman explain, "When a player makes a choice within a game, the action that results from the choice has an outcome. In Chess, if a player moves a piece on the board, this action affects the relationships of all of the other pieces."[32]

---

[32] Salen and Zimmerman, 56-67, 336-346; quotation from 33.

Making the results of player actions public (like moving a piece of a chessboard) provides two benefits. First, the player who took the action experiences positive feedback. Second, other players see the results as well. This spurs them to action. This is another good reason to make something like public voting your primary system. Everyone can see immediate results of their actions (even if some long term results remain concealed).[33]

This also encourages interaction. Making the resolution of player actions discernible to everyone helps all of the players develop situational awareness. Rewarding group actions with success actions encourages meaningful interactions between players.

Once again, this need for feedback is one reason voting is such a popular instrument in RTTP designs. Players have a choice presented to them. They vote. They immediately see the outcome, and they can note how others react to it. As is noted above, it may be desirable for their position on the first vote to be scripted. That way players can cast it with confidence. Later votes become more intellectually and politically complicated.

Players may also take actions privately. Some games feature binding agreements that can be made between players. For example, the First Grand Secretary in the *Confucianism* game possesses two tokens that allow him to give victory to other players. These tokens are validated by the GM. Other games have provisions for agreements between players and the GM. For example, the *Athens* game includes negotiations between one of the players and the Persians.

These are powerful instruments and they have the potential to reorganize the balance of the game. As a result, they can detract from your intellectual collisions. If the game is riddled with secret maneuverings everyone stops paying attention to the discussion.

---

[33] Salen and Zimmerman, 34-35.

Therefore, if you do make provisions for secret deals between players or between players and the GM, have them come to fruition towards the end of the game.

Maintaining a tight feedback loop may require a significant outlay of time on the part of the GM, but there are several good options for conveying feedback from the GM.

Many GMs send flurries of email immediately after each class session. These messages may be tips on the readings, scolds, or well-earned praise. Given the occasional emotional rawness that develops in RTTP, such notes are often a good idea, but they can create the impression among players that the GM is acting as a puppet-master.

During game sessions some GMs send handwritten notes to players for similar reasons. More obtrusive that the GM email, these prompts may be necessary to goad an inactive player, but even if they are distributed discreetly, most players track the passage of the note across the room with anxious eyes. Consequently, the use of such notes should be a personal choice. Avoid requiring it of your GMs.

Opening and closing announcements from the "GM News Service" may be the best device for conveying results of player actions. Making an omnibus announcement allows GMs to combine the results of public actions and private actions. It also allows for some degree of guidance/correction through the use of injections or public adjustments to the game mechanism. When these are presented together, it helps to create a seamless sense of the game world.

Regardless of the form it takes, when feedback comes directly from the GM it must be unimpeachable. *Don't make the GM lie!* If players start to think the GM is "messing with them," they step out of the game and often become disengaged.

Problem solving

It is tempting to think of the game as a sandbox where the players can freely explore the historical setting you have developed, but this rarely results in the sharp intellectual collisions that benefit most learning objectives. If you just turn players loose with absolute freedom of action, many players become paralyzed with indecision while others take actions that are irrational, implausible, and excessively impulsive.

Consequently, you must give them problems that need to be solved. Since games fall flat if players do not recognize they need to make a decision, you must also make sure that players understand when these problems need solving.

Set game schedules may seem constraining, but they give players some structure to operate in and greatly reduce player uncertainty about the moments when important choices are laid before them. If they know a decision must be made about a certain issue at a specific moment in the game, the presence of choice becomes clear.

Your schedule maps your planned collisions and the documents are the fuel, but it is not until players have objectives that they get the car on the road. Once they arrive at the problem you want them to have, give them the freedom and intellectual resources they need to solve it, but make sure that the problem they are solving is *your* problem. Furthermore, make sure the game mechanism provides them with a clear way to solve it.

Players must have a basic understanding of the game mechanism in order to know *how* to act upon their choices. If players have the opportunity to vote, they need to know voting procedures. If they may riot, they need to know how to instigate a riot. Otherwise, they will come up with all sorts of crazily implausible solutions.

If the structure requires certain player-generated events to take place in order to advance the game towards new problems, make sure that you assign this responsibility to multiple roles. Building in redundancy helps ensure that the event will occur, and it minimizes the need for GM interventions. For example, in *Forest Diplomacy* the Lt. Governor must give an oratory at a particular point in the game. If this oratory is not given, it creates confusion. Consequently, the role sheet of another role, Richard Peters, explains that he must take steps to make sure the Lt. Governor is prepared to present this oratory. In the unlikely event that he also fumbles, a third role, the Irish Trader, is charged with picking up the pieces with an *ad hoc* oratory. The game must go on.

Another way to build in redundancy is to make roles with positional leadership less secure. That way, if a player in a key position is not meeting the obligations of the role, the GM can arrange a substitution. In *Acid Rain and the European Environment, 1979-89* the UN Representative is a crucial role. It is not always possible to anticipate how well the player assigned the role will perform, so the role is assigned only for the first two game sessions, and the player is warned that the UN Secretary General (the GM) is prepared to dispatch a replacement if the Representative's work is unsatisfactory.

The Plausibility Corridor

In order for a game to work, players must have real choices. If they do not, they become disinterested and disengaged fairly quickly. Similarly, if the decisions they are making feel scripted or forced, the game may fail. In comparing games to set narratives, game theorist Greg Costikyan put it this way:

> Games are inherently non-linear. They depend on decision-making. Decisions have to pose, real, plausible alternatives, or they aren't real decisions. It must be entirely reasonable for a player to make a decision one way in one game, and a different way in the next. To the

degree that you make a game more like a story – more linear, fewer real options—you make it less like a game.[34]

This can create real tension for a designer, particularly if you know your historical material quite well. Designing a game that may deviate from historical outcomes is disturbing to many scholars who have laboriously constructed a detailed and nuanced understanding of a particular period or event. Yet, if a game design provides no opportunities for deviation from historical actuality it will fail.

Even so, player options must be circumscribed so they do not make choices that result in truly odd or implausible outcomes. Much of the art of designing a good RTTP game is creating a structure that imposes reasonable restraints while preserving enough freedom to engage the players.[35] Setting the width of such a historical Plausibility Corridor is a designer's choice, but its existence must be conveyed by the game – particularly if historical outcomes of the events modeled in the game are likely to be familiar to the players. They must understand that they may find Socrates innocent as long as they have historically plausible reasons for doing so. Generally, players accept limits on their actions, as long as they still possess an extensive set of options and do not feel railroaded into certain positions, but they will always attempt to bend these limits to their advantage.

The Plausibility Corridor creates the mental space for the game to take place. It gives the players a place to *play.* Salen and Zimmerman see it this way,

---

[34] Greg Costikyan, "I Have No Words & I Must Design." Originally published in *Interactive Fantasy* 2 (1994). Revised and published to the web at: http://www.costik.com/nowords2002.pdf. par. 28.
[35] Salen and Zimmerman, 66-67, 69.

Game designers do not directly design play. They only design the structures and contexts in which play takes place, indirectly shaping the actions of the players. We call the space of future action implied by a game design the *space of possibility.* [36]

The existence of this space is part of the genius of RTTP. It animates players to "improve" upon the historical outcome (at least as they see it from the point of view of their roles). In order to make these improvements plausible, they must understand the limits placed on their actions by the historical situation. Grasping the various available courses of action deepens their understanding of the historical moment gives them a sense of historical contingency. Together, these create a real sense of historical dynamism that is often lost in more traditional approaches to the study of the past.

In RTTP this space initially gets defined by the gamebook, but it takes on meaning only when the players begin interacting with the game mechanism and one another in meaningful ways. Designing the proper balance between possibility and chaos is difficult. It requires a well-designed and carefully calibrated game mechanism, and developing these usually requires extensive playtesting, which often reveals player strategies that result in historically implausible outcomes.

As the game progresses, the decisions that players take should open up new possibilities. This keeps the situation dynamic and reminds players that their actions matter. However, with each decision that gets made, the game may push further from historical actuality. In considering this, think about how far you are willing for the game to depart from history. How wide is your Plausibility Corridor? If there are issues that create a high likelihood for

---

[36] Salen and Zimmerman, 67.

dramatically ahistorical outcomes, put them near the end of the game to minimize the skew or include some instrument that will pull the action back on to the path of historical actuality.

When considering the shape of your decision tree keep the experience of the players in mind. Players generally do not care how broad the tree becomes, or how much it deviates from history, as long as victory remains possible.

If decisions are made early in the game which make it impossible for certain roles to win, those players become detached from the game. There are at least three ways to deal with this problem, but they all have possible drawbacks:

Persistence. Keep a major issue in play until the end of the game. *Possible drawback:* players feel powerless to resolve anything.

Injections. Change the situation to push the game back into the realm of historical possibility. *Possible drawback:* successful players may believe this devalues their earlier accomplishments.

Gradualism. Compartmentalize decisions so that there is not a branching decision tree. Instead, there is a checklist. *Possible drawback:* the game may lack dynamism.

Injections

Some events that are critical to the pacing, action, and outcome of the game are not determined by player action or the functioning of the game mechanism. Rather than being generated by player action, they are scripted into the structure of the game; this can be useful for several reasons:

- Maintaining historical accuracy
- Recalibrating discussion of an issue to new circumstances
- Introducing a new issue or secondary system

In all these cases, they can necessitate the reshuffling of relationships between players.

The easiest approach to introducing external events is through the use of announcements from the "GM News Service." For example, *Patriots, Loyalists & Revolution in New York City, 1775-76,* is structured by a series of injections describing outside New York City. These shape the context for players to make decisions. They also, in some cases, create a sense of urgency. *The British are coming!*

In addition to making quick public announcements, the GM provides more detailed briefings to a player who acts as a newspaper publisher. That player then has the responsibility to more fully explain the shifts in the situation through a publication.

Small, one-day demi-roles played by visitors to the class require less obvious GM intervention. These roles often act as provocateurs. In *Greenwich Village* a *New York Times* reporter demi-role allows the appearance of a point of view that is not shared by any other roles. This is usually played by the GM, but it can be easily taken up by a special guest.

Demi-roles may also act as new indeterminates who need to be persuaded. The final day of *Modernism vs. Traditionalism: Art in Paris, 1888-89,* features the display of works of art by the players who must convince the people playing demi-roles of various period art collectors to buy their art. This provide players with the opportunity to explain their aesthetics to people outside of the game, which creates a pedagogical capstone to the experience.

Surprise alterations of the scenario can be pedagogically useful, but if mishandled they may derail the game. If they appear to benefit some players more than others, they create resentment among the players who think they are now at a disadvantage.

Injections can also be distracting. If your game calls for request announcements, everyone starts looking for the next surprise instead of playing the game. They begin waiting for the

GM to make announcements rather than interacting with one another.

Consequently, it is usually best to give players fair warning. If a big shift in the game is coming, let them know so they can make contingency plans. Alternatively, you may want to force players to rely upon their knowledge of the historical context to assess and anticipate the potential for the intervention of external forces in the game. For example, the materials for the *Athens* game do not emphasize the strong possibility of Spartan intervention if Athens begins to remilitarize – it relies on players to introduce this possibility into the debates of the Assembly. If they fail to make this point strongly enough, the game may end with invasion.[37]

Regardless of their level of foreknowledge, consider giving players some influence over the specific form of the external events. Possessing some ability to alter injections is more satisfying than a bolt from the blue. It confirms player agency.

Game designer Tracy Fullerton provides some useful advice on how to bring external events into a game without destroying the players' sense that their actions matter.

> A good rule of thumb is to caution your players at least three times before hitting them with anything catastrophic. Random events that have a lesser impact require smaller warnings or even no warning at all. ... If you follow this rule, the events won't appear to be arbitrary and your players will feel like they are in control of their destiny.[38]

If you introduce an injection without any warning whatsoever, try to put it at the end of the game. *Greenwich Village* does this with a "false ending." Players think the game is over until the GM announces that there is another session that is set after the United

---

[37] Fullerton, 336.
[38] Fullerton, 336-337.

States entered the First World War. In this new context, players are forced to reevaluate their positions. The game is fundamentally changed by the heightened wartime repression, and that is exactly the point. So, *Greenwich Village* does it right – a massive injection blindsides the players, but it does so to teach a powerful lesson. Furthermore, it comes at the very end of the game, so it does not habituate players to dramatic interventions.

If you introduce external events, it is usually best to do so in a predetermined sequence laid out in the IM. Otherwise, an inexperienced GM may have difficulty bringing them into the game. This sequence may be concealed from the players, but the GM should be given clear direction. Alternatively, you may want to make injections optional. If you do this, use the IM to make it clear when and why certain injections should be used.

Recordkeeping

Once the game begins, things often move quite quickly. Players start taking actions. They pass laws; they make deals; they plot and scheme. Only some player actions need to be recorded, but players and GMs often become so caught up in the action that they forget to write things down.

Consequently, it is important to design recordkeeping instruments for the players and the GM to consult as the game proceeds. This is usually a brief record of key moments in the operation of the game mechanism. Depending on the game, it might be a record of votes, a compendium of laws, or the results of military actions.

If most (or all) important player actions are public it is easy to keep record-keeping transparent. Many games include the creation of laws. Posting these laws is a good way to remind everyone of what transpired in previous sessions. If there are only a few public things to record, then record-keeping seems easy because everyone can keep track of the records. However, most of the notes are fragmentary and even more confoundingly, most of the note-takers have incentives to fabricate their records. This might be a teachable moment that addresses one of your learning objectives (as is the case in *Forest Diplomacy*), but it may also be pretty annoying.

So, if possible, keep the voting mechanism simple. If you cannot do so, provide a worksheet for the GM. Additionally, consider tasking certain players with the responsibility of keeping records. Making these players biased can add an additional dimension to the game, but if all you need is reliable records, then make some roles into impartial historian/banker/scribes. This ensured that there is a written record kept by someone *other than* the GM. This relieves the GM of this responsibility or, at least, provides a check for it. A good example of this is *Greenwich Village*, which features a role, Polly, with a primary function as a record-keeper.

Tokens and artifacts can be very useful for recordkeeping. As the authors of *Gamestorming* note, "The more information you can store in material objects or the environment, the more your players' minds are free to engage with the situation at hand."[39] Tangible objects simplify recordkeeping because everyone can see and touch the record.

In *The Second Crusade: The War Council of Acre, 1148,* the GM distributes "holy relics" to players who present particularly strong speeches. These relics are proudly displayed by players who may, in turn, create reliquaries to house them. When the reliquaries are displayed, it acts as a force multiplier – reliquaries make the relics they house more powerful. These tokens are distributed and validated by the GM.

---

[39] Dave Gray, Sunni Brown, & James Macunfo, *Gamestorming: A Playbook for Innovators, Rulebreakers, and Changemakers* (Sebastopol, CA: O'Reilly Media, 2010), 18.

Other artifacts are created by the players themselves. Most commonly, these are laws. When ancient Athenians made laws, they were chiseled into stone, so players in the *Athens* game create laws, they are written on paper which is prominently posted for future reference. Like the reliquaries, these provide a visual record of the progress of the game. In addition, they direct the action of later stages of the game. The first law to be passed, the "Reconciliation Agreement" places limits on some of the discussions later in the game. As more laws are passed, the intellectual terrain becomes more complicated by the shared past of the game.

If the game includes a climax, records often become critically important because they often modify the terms of the final debates. Make sure that the GM can easily corral all of this information in anticipation of this final session so that it goes smoothly. Having GMs perform calculations on the fly quickly becomes taxing and it potentially raises the specter of an unjust or arbitrary GM. [40]

Rules-sanctioned secret deals between players can have a noticeable impact on the game mechanism, but in the confusion of the latter sessions of the game they are easy for the GM to forget. Consequently, if your game includes this sort of thing, you should provide the players and the GM with worksheets to record the specifics of these deals. Also provide a clear way to calculate the effects of these deals in the IM, so the GM does not need to calculate results on the fly.

Game fatigue

By the middle of the game, players understand the context, their roles and the intellectual collisions that drive the game. Some players become emotionally exhausted. Some of those doing well, become complacent and overconfident. Those doing poorly

---

[40] Greenblat, 64.

become frustrated and disengaged. Finally, if they think they have puzzled out the functioning of the game *as a game,* they become sloppy or bored. So, in order to keep these sessions of the game in motion, you need to shake things up.

The biggest problem is "lockup." This occurs when players build a faction into a permanent majority. Ideally, the dynamic of RTTP games is coalition-building rather than alliance-building. In other words, roles should be able to come into alignment on some issues, but they should find themselves in opposition on others. Creating small, stable alliances, like factions, can be good for the game, but if players can build an alliance that acts as a permanent majority the game may collapse.

When a permanent majority rules, attempts to persuade give way to stable voting blocs, and the intellectual center of the game – persuasion – withers. Plentiful indeterminate roles provide the best defense against lockup, but a good design includes other elements that prevent this from happening as well.

Holding off on decisions about certain issues until towards the end of the game can be a good way to break lockup. The climax of the *Athens* game is a trial of Socrates, and it is here that the Radical Democrats and the Moderate Democrats usually part ways. Similarly, in *Kentucky 1861,* the issue of secession finally comes to fruition towards the end of the game. This forces a reshuffling of coalitions.

Other approaches are conveyed through injections that alter the context for the game. In *Patriots, Loyalists & Revolution in New York City,* the announcement of Dunmore's Proclamation (an offer by the Governor of Virginia to free slaves who fight for the Crown), new opportunities arise for slave players. This often disrupts alliances that they formed in the early stages of the game with patriots.

Some injections introduce new secondary systems. This can be a good addition if players begin devoting more energy to vote counting than persuasion. A new secondary system can alter the situation enough to require the players to consider things from a new perspective. It may also encourage them to realign themselves into new coalitions.

Murder

Some players will attempt to shift the action of game with murder. Given the opportunity, many players gravitate toward violence. Most players think that this is a fun part of the game. They also like murder because it is a straightforward solution. Rather than persuading others to adopt their positions, some would rather simply remove those who do not agree with them.

As a result, if there is the opportunity to kill, many players cease thinking about the intellectual collisions. They even cease thinking about game politics. They just think about how to kill one another. Consequently, only add murder to your game if it actually addresses one of your learning objectives. It is important for players to spend most of the time engaging one another with ideas rather than threats, so weigh the costs and benefits very carefully.

Furthermore, you should only add the possibility of violence if there is strong historical evidence that it influenced the intellectual collisions that your game focuses upon. The potential for personal violence is often present in historical moments that feature stark and spirited disagreement, but it often does not alter the tenor of the discussions. So, I agree with Mark Carnes who remarked, "I think that unless there is a strong possibility of assassination, as evidenced by the historical record, it should be discouraged."[41]

---

[41] Mark Carnes in "Reacting to the Past Faculty Lounge" Facebook group, April 11, 2012.

However, there can be good reasons for making killing part of your game. Violent acts were an essential part of the growing strength of the patriot cause in the period examined by *Patriots, Loyalists & Revolution in New York City,* so the author, Bill Offutt, made it an integral part of the game. As such, the game carefully lays out the mechanics and function of violence. It also provides clear rules for the "resurrection" of eliminated players with new roles. Clear mechanics are key because when violence comes into the game it is invariably accompanied by excitement and emotions.

Mexico in Revolution, 1911-1920, features a great deal of violence, so the designers, Jonathan Truitt and Stephany Slaughter, have added a number of features to the game in order to prevent the violence from spiraling totally out of control. First, they recommend that any assassinations should happen at the end of class. This maximizes the time in which the eliminated player has to learn a new role. Second, the game provides a host of back-up roles with clear objectives and strong incentives for re-entering the game. Give these roles exciting special powers. This helps to salve the pain of virtual death. If the new roles lack these, eliminated players often remain detached from the game. Other times they re-enter the game with a fury, but only because they continue to play their initial role. In these cases, their primary motivation becomes revenge.[42]

If you do make killing an option, try to provide easier ways for players to achieve the same ends. In addition (or alternatively) create preconditions that must be met before a murder may be attempted. If players need to achieve an intermediate goal before they can proceed to an actual assassination attempt, it reduces the level of disruption and it provides a check on players who want to kill someone "because it seems fun."

---

[42] Jon Truitt outlined several of these ideas in the "Reacting to the Past Faculty Lounge" Facebook group, April 11, 2012.

Endgame

Ideally, your game will come to some sort of final climactic showdown. This keeps the players involved through the end, provides some resolution to major conflicts, and heightens emotional involvement in the game.

Ending the game is a delicate matter because, as Greenblat points out, "It is important to guard against artificial ends of play (endgame strategies). Sometimes the end is obvious and reasonable: a period of time is given to the culminating parliamentary session, and play ends when the decision is reached; a vote is taken to see who has won the election." But, even in these cases, it is important to guard against players taking advantage of the "end-of-the-world" (e.g. backstabbing everybody at the last minute).[43] If military action is possible, the best way to avoid last minute suicidal charges is to construct objectives that encourage the preservation of forces. Similarly, if your game mechanism includes some form of currency, create some benefit for not spending everything at the last minute.

Alternatively, you may want to provide for an abrupt ending. If the game suddenly ends when everyone is planning their last moves, they will be disappointed, but you avoid the implementation of endgame strategies. You can always use the post-game discussion for examining "what would have happened if..."

Regardless of the exact form of the end of the game, many players become depressed and demoralized after a game ends, so it can be good to usher them outside the magic circle and back into the real world with a social event. Watch a movie about the period your game covered. Go out to eat at an appropriate restaurant. Burn someone in effigy.

---

[43] Greenblat, 63.

6. Reflection: Debriefing the game

Just as designers neglect the initial stage of setting learning objectives, most GMs set aside insufficient time for reflection. Marieke Kleiboer's assessment of the importance of this stage for crisis simulations also applies to RTTP:

> Systematic feedback to participants is a crucial aspect of simulations ... For the analyst, the feedback stage is a chance to obtain participants' recommendations for improving the simulation. For the participants themselves, the feedback stage provides an opportunity to review and evaluate their own behavior, explain the reasoning behind their actions during the simulations and discuss the problems and frictions encountered during the simulation. Participants should be given a clear review of the strengths and weaknesses of their performance during the simulation.[44]

Since everyone will have different learning experiences make sure that you allot sufficient time for them to share their experiences in the post-game debriefing. This will enrich everyone's experience.[45]

---

[44]Marieke Kleiboer, "Simulation Methodology for Crisis Management Support," *Journal of Contingencies and Crisis Management,* vol. 5, no. 4 (1997), 205.
[45] Greenblat, 63.

Indeed, this may be the most significant stage of your game in terms of learning. Do not sell it short. Players need an opportunity to come out of the game and to relate to one another outside of their roles. Give them this time.

Some players have difficulty leaving the game behind. Mark Carnes regularly experiences difficulty when he asks students to put aside their roles. During the debriefing, when he asks students "who was on the right side" in the game, they quickly revert to arguments they made in the game. A student usually makes note of this, which Carnes follows by asking, "If you have come to believe things that you've been assigned to believe within one month, think of all of the unexamined ideas that you've been living with for all of your life." This can be a significant and teachable moment. As he notes, "We teach students that, when motivated, they can find arguments to support all sorts of ideas; but I think that we show how easy it is to persuade yourself of your own views – even when you're wrong." A discussion featuring these insights may help realize his hope that "by having multiple identities and ideas percolating in students' minds, they will be less rigid intellectually."[46]

In addition to providing time for players to reflect on their experiences, debriefing must include an opportunity for the GM to clarify the ahistorical points of the game while describing the actual events that occurred. A good IM provides post-game discussion prompts for all of this, and they should be tied back into the overarching learning objectives of the game. In the excitement of the final sessions, everyone (including the GM) often lose track of these; the debriefing is essential to bring everyone back to the learning objectives.

---

[46] Mark Carnes, Reacting to the Past Faculty Lounge, Facebook group, Aug. 6, 2012.

7. Chapter Games

A chapter game is a short RTTP game. Excluding setup and debriefing, a chapter game can be played in as few as three hours. These could be continuous, but breaking up the run of a game into several discrete sessions allows the players more time to process the ideas and to engage in intrigue. The brevity of these games means that they must be designed particularly carefully in order to engage players quickly and with a minimum of confusion. For example, in long games, players have sufficient time to become comfortable with their roles, but this time is not available in a chapter game.[47]

Game elements

A debate between two sides attempting to appeal to a jury of indeterminates is a good and useful pedagogical tool, but it is not – strictly speaking – an RTTP game. In order to remain inside the Reacting tent, chapter games must include the essential elements of RTTP games that are described in chapter one.

---

[47] This chapter draws heavily on a handful of unpublished game designs and my conversations and correspondence with their creators. They include, J. Patrick Coby, *Launching the Ship of State: Ratification Debates in New York State, 1788,* ver., 4 Feb. 2013; Tony Crider, *The Pluto Debate;* David Henderson and Susan Henderson, *Challenging the USDA Food Pyramid,* ver. 2.1; Gretchen McKay, *The Iconoclastic Controversy in Byzantium, 726-843*; Jeff Hyson, *Making a Motion Picture Production Code.*

In addition, chapter games must have the same components (gamebooks, role sheets, and instructor's manuals) as full-length games, but the contents of each may be a little different. For example, chapter games may not need vignettes. In addition, much of the reading for chapter games can appear in companion volumes or stable Internet links. For example, the gamebook for Tony Crider's *Pluto Debate* is two pages long and role sheets are only one page long, but all of the roles are instructed to complete assignments using online resources and several chapters in a companion book. Full-length games, by contrast, tend to include everything one needs to play the game as part of the game materials.

Even with simplification and focus, a single session of game play only allows players the opportunity to deal with a single issue in any depth. Thus, a one-day exercise that includes RTTP elements is best characterized as a *debate*. In order for many of the game-like qualities of RTTP to enter into the equation, players need at least two and probably three sessions that are separated from one another in time. This is because, in order to play a game, players need time for informal interactions; these are essential for deal-making, coalition-building, and GM consultations. If they are not able to do these things, they can still have an intellectually stimulating exchange of ideas, but they will not have the opportunity for these interactions to become a game.

Furthermore, even though chapter game roles are shorter and more circumscribed than those in full-length games, they do have multiple dimensions, which become apparent through interacting with other players. If these never take place, the roles become fairly superficial.

Consequently, RTTP chapter games customarily have two to three sessions of game play along with time for setup and debriefing. Since it takes time for players to enter into their roles, it is usually best to introduce them before the game begins in earnest. If players receive their roles before they start doing the background reading, they have time to start thinking in terms of their roles. It also gives keen players an opportunity to begin lobbying indeterminates, organizing faction meetings or identifying potential allies and enemies. If they receive their roles too close to the beginning of the game, players spend a lot of the first session trying to remember their identities and objectives. Full-length games allow players time enough to become comfortable with their roles but chapter games require greater urgency.

Scripting for clarity

Simplicity and clarity are always good characteristics for a game mechanism because they prevent confusion. This allows players to concentrate on playing the game and engaging in the intellectual collisions that the game is designed to create rather than trying to figure out how to play. The need for these qualities is intensified by the brevity of chapter games. The collision of ideas must begin right away, and it must not relent until the end of the game. To facilitate this, these games need to be somewhat scripted.

To this end, players need to know when they need to make decisions or take action. Susan and David Henderson's *Challenging the USDA Food Pyramid, 1991,* is a good example of a well-structured chapter game because it concludes with two votes, which are followed by die rolls that determine the outcome for indeterminates. This focuses the arguments throughout the game on these final decisions. Thus, members of factions know what they need to focus on in order to win votes, while indeterminates know what is at stake when they listen to the arguments. By keeping everything in flux until the end of the game, this structure keeps everyone engaged.

Resolutions should be prewritten and included in the gamebook and IM. They should not be subtle. Everyone should fully understand their impact and meaning. For example, my own three-session *Chicago, 1968,* which is set in the Democratic National Convention, ends each session with a vote. The first session addresses the domestic policy portion of the party platform. The second session addresses Vietnam, and at the end of the third session delegates select their nominee for president. In each case, rather than drawing up the wording themselves, delegates choose from a selection of pre-written statements that appear in the gamebook. This allows the players to argue the merits of different positions instead of getting bogged down in word-smithing. This keeps them focused on the learning objectives of the game.

Along the same lines, the topics and timing of speeches, votes, and other important actions should be pre-set and the schedule should be in the gamebook, IM, and pertinent role sheets. Everyone should know when they are supposed to speak and the topic they are supposed to speak about. Furthermore, they should have a pretty good idea what everyone else is going to speak about.

All of this helps to make the intellectual collisions clear. The gamebook for Patrick Coby's *Launching the Ship of State* focuses players on a handful of ideas when it states, "Only one constitutional issue will engage you: the qualities and obligations of elected officials (lower-house representatives especially) and the structural elements needed to elect and control such persons."[48] This is just a small slice of the historical debates over the ratification of the constitution, but without these limits the debate would become unmanageable; if unrestrained, knowledgeable players would bring a host of other issues into the game and the learning objectives would be lost in a blizzard of historical references. Players would talk past each other.

---

[48] J. Patrick Coby, *Launching the Ship of State: Ratification Debates in New York State, 1788,* ver. 4 Feb. 2013.

This direction means that players do not have the opportunity to discover the full dimensions of the disagreements between Federalist and Anti-Federalist, but this focus on a subset of these ideas allows them to quickly focus and to concentrate on the issues that lie before them.

A full-length RTTP game is like a great estate, filled with rambling trails, grand promenades, stands of ancient trees, and delightful, burbling brooks. Chapter games are carefully tended gardens with straight pathways, row crops, gates, and fences. They are both beautiful expressions of the gardener's art, but they are quite different in form, execution, and purpose.

Some gardens are overgrown. Designers who convert full-length games to chapter games often retain more issues from the full game than can be accommodated in their limited agenda of a chapter game. This might allow heavy-handed GMs to focus the game on the issues that are of most interest to them. They can plow some furrows before the game begins.

Alternatively, some GMs allow a free-for-all in which players struggle to get their issues addressed. In these cases, getting on the agenda becomes an objective in itself. Tracy Lightcap sees this as a positive because it reflects reality. "In actual policy situations," he writes, "people must be persuaded and the first step is often to get them to care one way or another about the issues being faced."[49] However, this can be tricky.

If players are boxed out early in the game and it becomes clear that the issues that are most important to them will not be addressed, it increases the chances that they will withdraw from the game or, more disruptively, seek to break it. Consequently, the free-for-all option is best utilized only when the struggle to define the agenda is one of the learning objectives for the game itself.

---

[49] Lightcap.

Some designers are reluctant to script their games to this extent because doing so quashes the potential for player innovation. This is a legitimate concern because the focus required to make chapter games work allows fewer opportunities for exploration and discovery. However, these games remain intellectually rich because players must still contend with one another. The presence of indeterminates and opponents and the existence of a game mechanism make the players think creatively about structuring their arguments, arranging evidence, engaging in skullduggery, and interacting with other players.

As long as you only script the elements that are *essential* to the functioning of the game, players retain a significant amount of agency; but do not forget that they only have a couple sessions to get where they need to go. As fun as it might be to have them wander far afield, pulled hither and yon by whim and curiosity, they need to keep their eyes on the prize. They must cross the intellectual terrain that you intend. Making sure they do not drive to Mexico is different from forbidding innovation.[50]

Orienting the players

Players must understand their roles in order to enter into the game. In a chapter game they do not have much time to orient themselves to one another and the game mechanism once the game begins. Consequently, they must be oriented *before* the game begins. In order for this to work, the game mechanism, their place within it, and the relationship of players to one another must all be simple and straightforward.

If players are familiar with the roles, arguments, and context this orientation can be quite brief. As Tony Crider explains, "it takes most students several game sessions to get into character for *Trial of Galileo*; they don't understand the era or the arguments."

---

[50] Email from Gretchen McKay, April 24, 2013.

Knowing this, he designed the first act of his *Pluto Debate* chapter game to build on what players already probably know about the issues in the game. Consequently, he's found that students are able to enter into the game about 10-20 minutes into the first session.[51]

In terms of quick orientation, clear and straightforward objectives are a must. Players do not have time to figure out how to translate vague objectives into game terms. They need clearly defined objectives.

In a chapter game there is not enough time for the GM to reset the game when overly optimistic players create an implausible compromise. Therefore, if you want them to engage in a spirited and adversarial discussion, make it clear that a compromise solution is not possible. Instead, focus them on the challenge of persuading indeterminates.

As is noted above, this means that game mechanics must be exceptionally clear and easy to understand. They should be free of time-consuming protocols. If, for example, things are decided by voting, script the timing and topic of the votes, and make the GM responsible for totaling them.

In order to ensure the smooth functioning of the game mechanism, have the GM select presiding officers before gameplay begins. As is the case with full-length games, these players should have deputies in case they fail to show up. In some cases, it may even be beneficial to make the GM into a presiding officer – provided the role is an impartial one.

Players need to understand their relationship of to one another before the game begins. Players will not have time to discover the subtle constellations of power and influence that often appear in full-length games, so they must understand the political situation before the game even begins. The most straightforward way to do this is by placing *all* of the players into factions. *For, Against,* and

---

[51] Email from Tony Crider, April 18, 2013.

Undecided can be a good breakdown of factions. In addition to simplifying the political situation, putting every player into a faction provides everyone with a built-in support network.

Avoid having unique players with esoteric objectives. A chapter game does not give someone playing this sort of role enough time to figure out how to relate to other players or how to enter the game. If you must have some quirky roles, clone them; that way everyone has a buddy.

Keep the relationships between players solid. To this end, it is probably best to forbid defections from factions. This gives players a foundation of trust and certainty in what can be as bewildering a situation as a full-length game. When someone you thought was your friend walks away in pursuit of individual victory, it can lead to out-of-game acrimony. If disloyal faction members are a necessary component of your game – perhaps you want to show how a coalition breaks down when the issues change – then make sure other faction members are able to see it coming. If players know why people defect in game terms, they are less likely to hold it against them personally.

Basically, avoid nasty surprises. This follows the advice of Tony Crider, who explained, "You can still have a complex discussion about the topics, but you don't need (and don't have time for) the complex rules and twists of a standard Reacting game."[52]

Since players will not have sufficient time to puzzle out secret agendas or to put together conspiracies, the vast majority of their objectives should be public knowledge. Chapter games are not the place for secrets. Hidden agendas work in full-length games because there is sufficient time for them to be discovered (or at least suspected), but in a chapter game they are a distraction from the central issues. Players need to be focused on the intellectual

---

[52] Tony Crider, "Reacting to the Past Faculty Lounge," Facebook group, August 9, 2012.

collisions. They must know where they stand on the issues and they must understand when they need to act.

Persuasion is a key element of RTTP; it depends on the existence of players who are indeterminate, or undecided, about certain issues. In full-length games these players have the opportunity to let their roles ripen over the course of the game. They are also free to follow more independent paths than players who are in factions. The brevity of chapter games prohibits such freedoms. They need to have clear choices put before them, and by the end of the game they must align themselves in terms of the central questions in the game.

In order to make this an informed decision, indeterminates need to fully understand the nature of their indeterminacy. Why are they indeterminate? Why will they need to stop being indeterminate? What do they want to hear? What do they *not* want to hear? Aside from persuasion, they need to know how the game mechanism can allow them to achieve victory.

All of this is necessary because if indeterminates do not have rules that set the terms of their indeterminacy these players are prone to make alignments based upon pre-existing relationships with other players. Alternatively, they might align out of ignorance or on a whim. These are not desirable outcomes.

Courting indeterminates should be fairly straightforward as well. Members of factions need to know who the indeterminates are and they need some advice about how to lobby them. Sometimes, indeterminates attempt to form a "third faction." If this option is legitimate, simply design a third faction yourself. If this option is illegitimate, require indeterminates to align themselves with one of the existing factions.

Game or debate?

There are several ways in which one can construct a chapter game to ensure that it works as a game rather than as a debate. The first is to include at least two different issues. This adds a political element to the persuasion of indeterminates. The potential for vote trading and other barrel-rolling agreements encourage players to interact with one another. If there is a single issue, there is more potential for a majority of indeterminates to decide their loyalties early in the game, which can make the rest of the game seem futile. The addition of a second issue facilitates realignment, and this keeps everyone on their toes.

Games may also benefit from the addition of a single secondary system. But unlike the secondary systems in full-length games, which may only be fully understood by a handful of players, in a chapter game, secondary systems should be understood by everyone. Consequently, it is best to keep them as public as is possible. Even if all the players are not able to directly participate in the system, the ways in which it functions should be made clear in the gamebook and role sheets. In addition to providing transparency, this approach facilitates interaction.

Another easy way to shake a debate into a game is through the use of a scripted injection that changes the terms of the debate. The same principle is true for full-length games, but (as with everything else) in a chapter game it must be more carefully done. There should probably only be a single injection and it should be clearly defined as such. It can provide a good pivot from one issue to the next. Ideally, it comes at a break between sessions. This gives players time to digest the information and think about the implications of the new situation.

Climax

Even more than full-length games, chapter games should build to a climax. Their brevity allows the focus to remain on a final showdown. This can keep everyone energized for the entire game. In order for this to work, every role must be able to influence the outcome of the climax in some way. Postponing the achievement of ultimate victory until the very end of the game keeps everyone active. However, this can result in players seeing earlier decisions as low stakes. If players save up their energies and arguments for a final *big push* at the end of the game, it may be exciting, but the early part of the game may become dull and superficial.

Consequently, make sure that decisions that are made earlier in the game influence the outcome of the climax. This honors the efforts of players who worked hard in the early phases of the game, while preventing them from resting on their laurels. In fact, it may make them more energized in the later stages of the game because they will not want to throw away the victory for which they have laid a solid foundation. Simultaneously, this keeps players who have taken their lumps in the early game active. They possess the ability to win a stunning upset or a dramatic come-from-behind victory. None of this will work if players do not recognize the possibility of victory, so it is important to make the stakes of the final decision(s) very high and to convey this in the gamebook and role sheets.

Multiple games

Acquainting players with playing games is often the biggest challenge to using RTTP. The need to get players accustomed to playing a role and interacting with other players can be a time-consuming process (especially when they lack much knowledge about the topic of the game). Fortunately, full-length games provide enough time to ease into a game. Chapter games lack this luxury, but RTTP instructors have noticed that there is a learning curve; it gets easier for players to make this adjustment when they play multiple games.

David Henderson has found "that for each successive short game I used, the students got involved faster and immersion was deeper. … When students encounter RTTP for the first time, they are confused. … I think a major source of this confusion is just the very idea of doing games in class."[53]

This suggests the need for a large library of chapter games so that chapter games may be bundled together. However, the vagaries of academic calendars, curricula, and instructor preferences, mean that chapter games will be used in all sorts of ways. Consequently, even if players benefit from playing multiple games, each individual game must be designed for use in isolation.

[53] Email from David Henderson, April 19, 2013.

8. Scalability & Modifications

Instructors regularly modify RTTP games. They run games in small classes; they run games in big classes. They compress schedules and expand them. They mess around with the assignments. They drop in new readings, while they take others out. All of this can be vexing to designers of carefully crafted games, but designers must always be mindful and charitable of these instructors. The determination of these instructors to maintain the integrity of their classes must take precedence over the desire of designers to maintain the integrity to their games.

Many of the modifications that instructors make to games work well in the field, but they require time and effort to construct. Other modifications do not work well, which prevents the games from achieving their potential in terms of learning. These failures also sour people to the idea of RTTP. Providing assistance to these instructors by making the structure of games more flexible and by providing playtested variations to games that address a variety of common needs will serve the community well. This also reduces the likelihood that first time GMs will make ill-informed revisions that seriously damage games.

Number of players

RTTP games were originally designed to work in seminar courses with 18-25 players. Most students experience RTTP in courses of this size, but a growing number play games in large lecture courses. This presents a number of challenges.

The first is the limited time available for speaking during class sessions. The traditional RTTP two-speech structure simply cannot be accommodated, but without the opportunity for players to express their ideas, the intellectual collisions fall flat. Inventive instructors have developed several ways to deal with this problem by altering the structure of the speech assignments.

The Russian Roulette technique increases the size of the factions and then requires several players from each of them to prepare speeches for each session. (All of these speeches are accompanied by written papers, which are often posted on classroom management software before the game session.) At the beginning of the session, the GM selects the members of each faction who actually need to present their speeches from the podium. This approach ensures that players all grapple with the ideas because they must all prepare speeches. It also increases the likelihood of peer review because ambitious faction members will want to make sure that their allies present the faction position well.

Another approach calls for very rapid speeches. This technique requires players to write a lengthy paper, which expands upon the ideas in their speech, but it limits their time to present prepared remarks from the podium to a minute at most. This gets everyone up there, but it can lead to superficiality.

Another approach does away with prepared speeches altogether. Instead of outlining proposals and arguments from the podium, factions put together newspapers, which they must then publish electronically. When players mount the podium, they are prepared to answer questions, but the text of their proposals and the meat of their prepared arguments are only available in print. This maintains the time for verbal fencing in the form of spirited question and answer sessions, but it players do not read the publications carefully, the discussions fall flat.

These alterations open up more in-class time for the exchange of ideas, but in order for the game to operate *as a game,* players also need plenty of time for informal interactions. These are critical because deal-making is usually a significant part of the games. Given the lack of in-class time, the only solution here is to push more of these interactions outside of the regular class meetings.

The best solution in these cases is probably to expand and give more structure to the informal discussions that already happen. The easiest interactions to facilitate are those between members of the same faction. Members of these groups are usually keen to meet up with one another, but the scale of the class creates additional logistical problems, so the GM must be able to clear away some of the obstacles.

In the student survey that I conducted in 2013, I asked students "How did you interact with other players and the instructor?" They checked every answer that applied, and their responses are interesting.[54]

Class meetings	92 %
Out of class meetings	66 %
IMs	11 %
Texting	44 %
Email	79 %
Social media	39 %
Classroom management systems	25 %

This makes it evident that face-to-face meetings are ideal and that GM-created electronic spaces, such as classroom management systems, are comparatively underutilized. While texting and social media have high rates of participation, many of the players I've

---

[54] Scalability survey.

talked to explain that they primarily use these as scheduling tools when they attempt to put together face-to-face meetings.

Consequently, rather than calling for GMs to construct special electronic spaces for player interaction, the game materials should limit themselves to general suggestions about these spaces. Players will then follow through using the media best suited to their needs.

Factions seem to encounter the most difficulties when they attempt to divide tasks among the members. No one wants to seem bossy, so it can be helpful if the game materials make provisions for task specialization. This allows everyone to fall into certain slots fairly easily. Factions can be divided into all sorts of workgroups. Some might focus on lobbying certain indeterminates while others might draft important documents. Faction secretaries can be charged with disseminating minutes among faction members who could not attend meetings. Party whips can make sure that everyone knows how to vote on certain issues. There are plenty of jobs that need to be done if a large faction is going to function well. Help the players to get these sorted out so that they can start engaging the game instead of burning a lot of time sorting themselves out.

Indeterminates present more of a challenge, but there are ways to pull them into a large game too. The first of these requires detailing specific faction members to lobby certain indeterminates. This accelerates something that would probably happen anyway and it is simply done because it does not require a "big game" modification to the role sheets.

Another simple way to make provisions for indeterminates in large games is to clone indeterminate roles so that they become micro-factions. This gives players a peer group and a discussion section. Unanimous agreement between the clones is required before the indeterminate can take action. This technique gets indeterminates into the game, but it can be unsatisfying for players. Being "George Washington #3" is arguably less fun that playing a minor but individual role.

Another approach is to create more indeterminate roles that act primarily as observers rather than participants. Cast as historians, journalists, or scribes, these roles need to focus on the action because they have major writing assignments due at the end of the game. In order to complete the assignment, they need to give an account of the action that transpired over the course of the game. The documents that these roles create can add a lot to the debriefing.

While the accommodation of large classes is a growing issue, statistically, the more common problem is running RTTP games in small classes. 20% of the students I surveyed played games in classes with fifteen or fewer students.[55] In these games, the problems tend to be the inverse of large classes. There is too much time in plenary; there are too few speeches; lockup is more common because there are fewer indeterminates.

These cases are harder to accommodate. The best approach is probably to think about how to shrink the roster of roles down to eight to ten players, but with numbers that small, indeterminacy becomes difficult. The factions should wither in order to preserve as many indeterminate roles as possible, but that creates fragility too.

Scheduling

The second most common set of alterations concern scheduling. 16% of the students I surveyed reported that they played games with modified schedules.[56] Despite original plans for RTTP games to be played in 75 minutes sessions twice a week, they are now used in all sorts of formats ranging from 50 minute sessions that meet three times each week to 180 minute sessions that meet only

---

[55] Scalability survey.
[56] Scalability survey.

once per week. Since instructors are bound and determined to make the games work in these formats, game designers should provide them with as much help as possible.

As a general principle, the easiest way to aid GMs with scheduling is to organize games into *sessions* rather than *days* or *weeks.* Breaking the games into components allows greater flexibility when instructors need to scatter sessions across the calendar. An outline schedule should appear in the gamebook; dividing it into sessions will allow GMs to put the sessions into bundles.

Any particulars about the sessions should be included in the IM. Some sessions might be distinct elements of the game that can be cleaved from it. For example, if a game calls for opening introductions, those might be dealt with at the end of a setup day. Similarly, sessions that include a lot of injections or that typically have difficulty coming to a resolution should be flagged so that GMs make sure to allocate sufficient time to them.

Some sessions work best if some time passes between them. For example, in *Kentucky 1861,* Lincoln's first inaugural address appears as a mid-game injection. Players need significantly more time to read and digest this than any of the other injections in the game. So, if some time needs to pass between sessions, let the GMs know.

GMs also often need to compress games in order to fit them into their schedules. In order to aid them, flag critically important sessions as well as any that are less than critical. For example, *Forest Diplomacy* ordinarily includes three days of treaty negotiations. Eliminating the third day potentially creates some problems, but a canny GM can deal with them. Eliminating two of these days would destroy the game. GMs need to know this stuff.

Assignments

Assignments are the most commonly altered elements of RTTP games. 30% of the students I surveyed reported playing games with altered writing assignments, while 38% reported that they played games with reading assignments that differed from those outlined in the gamebook.[57]

Instructors regularly change the length, number, format, and content of these assignments in order to fit the learning objectives for their specific classes. For example, a writing intensive course might require formal essays, while a rhetoric course focused on oral communications might only require informal writing assignments, while placing greater expectations on speeches. A first year seminar might emphasize group work by making explicit provisions for peer review, while an upper level course might require the use of additional source materials as identified by independent research.

The best solution for this problem is to put all of the details about assignments in the IM. The gamebook and role sheets should retain references to speeches, essays, and newspapers, but they should be stripped of particulars. Instead of dictating a single version of these assignments, the IM should contain a handful of varied model assignments. These give instructors some help and inspiration in designing assignments to fit their classes. This way, the assignments players receive from the GM are uniform throughout the game materials. This reduces player confusion and makes things easier for the GM.

Modding

In addition to providing enough flexibility for instructors to alter games to fit the peculiarities of their classes, game designers should prepare themselves for the day when someone posts a

---

[57] Scalability survey.

modification that goes beyond formatting. Some GMs will actually start to change the content and mechanics of the game.

The development of RTTP modifications bears particular resemblance to electronic gaming community because RTTP games possess a number of similarities to open source software, which means that through careful reading and attentive play, GMs (and to some extent, players) can develop a full understanding of the game mechanism and the functions of all of the game components. This allows GMs to manipulate your game in fundamental ways. Most often, enterprising GMs create new roles and new secondary systems.

For example, when I co-taught the *Athens* game with a theater professor, we wanted to increase the role of ancient Greek drama in the game. To this end, we assigned a Sophocles play as additional required reading, wrote two new roles (a playwright and a leader of the chorus), and created a new secondary system, which bestowed extra votes upon the player elected best actor. Similarly, in an effort to broaden the coverage of the *Confucianism* game, I created three new roles. Two of them, the Student of Xunzi and the Daoist Jinshi, added two additional philosophies from the Ming era to the game debates. In addition, I wrote a third role, the Purist protégé, in an effort to tweak the game mechanism.

These sorts of modification are often posted to the RTTP Game Library, and they are healthy additions to the RTTP community. They keep the games new and they encourage innovation by faculty in the grassroots. In this, they are reflective of gaming communities in general. As game designer and design theorist Mary Flanagan notes, "Because they primarily exist as rule systems, games are particularly ripe for subversive practices."[58]

However, RTTP games are difficult to modify because the complexity and balance of the game mechanisms are often

---

[58] Flanagan, *11*.

obscured. Even after running or playing a game several times, you may not fully understand how the components should work in concert, but since people are inevitably going to modify your game, you should strive to make this process as easy as possible for them.

The upshot of this section is to convince you that regardless of the long hours you put into perfecting and fine-tuning your design, someone is eventually going to want to make modifications. There is no good reason to be obstructionist, and if you provide some designer's notes in the IM, they are less likely to severely imbalance the game mechanism.

9. Development

A completed game is one that can be managed by a GM who is not an expert in the content area of the game or in RTTP pedagogy. Getting your game design to this stage is neither easily nor quickly done.

Playtesting and dissemination

Playtesting is the gaming equivalent of sending an article out to peer readers, and putting together a group of playtesters is more challenging than finding peer readers because playtesters must allot a significant amount of time in their classes to make room for your game. Friends and colleagues are great playtesters because they will do this for you at an early stage, but remember that in order to develop your game fully, strangers must play it.

Since playtesting requires other people to make copies of your game, it is important for you to clearly understand your rights in publicizing and distributing your game in the various states of publication – including how you retain rights over the game (particularly copyright) when various versions of it are circulating around the Internet.

One way to simply and easily describe expectations for use is to place a Creative Commons license on your work. CC licenses were developed specifically with the intent of allowing content creators to retain copyright to their work while allowing others to use the work in various ways. Creating a CC license is an extremely easy process and should take no more than 3-5 minutes. It will allow you to think about your expectations for the work, answer questions about both non-commercial and commercial use of the work by others, and consider the possibility of derivative works created by others. Find the Creative Commons license chooser at: http://creativecommons.org/choose/

It is very straightforward, and it will produce a description of the license parameters you choose. You can then paste the text into your work. In addition, you should probably add a note about how you would like to receive feedback on your game. (For an example, see the second page of this handbook).

Playtests usually result in revisions, so figure out a good way to make sure your playtesters are using the most current version of the game. Perhaps you want to publish a new version on some sort of schedule.

You also may want to use a "versioning number" for your game. You can follow the model of software development, and start with 0.1 during testing, move to 0.2, 0.3, etc. and then release version 1.0 as your first "playable by others" game. You can then use 1.1, 1.2, etc. to make changes, and move to 2.0 when you make a major overhaul. If you pursue this course, change the numbering of every game element so that GMs know they have the most up to date version of everything.

Alternatively, you might want your numbering system to follow that of the RTTP development process. At present, games progress through the following stages:

1. **Concept.** Game materials are not fully developed by the author and/or the game has not been playtested by the author.
2. **Prototype.** Author designs and play-tests prototype game. Game materials are available from the author.

3. **Approved for playtesting.** Game materials are posted to online Forum where they can be downloaded for classroom use.
4. **Final review.** Game materials are posted in the online Forum where they can be downloaded for classroom use.
5. **Published.**

Some designers want to ensure that a small number of game manuals can be copied for educational use and while the copier can recoup the cost of copying, the games are not to be sold at a profit. This is certainly possible, although there is no specific CC licensing provision for this. You can simply add a statement onto the license that states that educators wishing to use the game for a course can make a small number of copies of the game and charge enough money for them to cover the costs of copying.

The bottom line is that licensing your work is an easy process, and more importantly, licensing is a necessary process to communicate with others your expectations for how your work will be used. Not understanding licensing or your own rights does not make the problem go away. Creative Commons is an easy way to define, design, and assign licenses to your work, but there are other mechanisms for licensing available to you as the author that you may want to investigate.[59]

Critique and feedback

Playtesting is at the center of the RTTP game development process, and focused feedback is essential to improving a game and moving it toward eventual publication. There are several groups of users from which you should gather feedback. The most common users are players and GMs, but other groups are

---

[59] Many thanks to Megan Squire for writing up an excellent description of Creative Commons, which served as the basis for this section. Hopefully, my editing did not greatly corrode the clarity of her ideas.

important too. Feedback from conference participants and preceptors can be very useful as well. Since the experiences and perspectives of each of these groups is somewhat distinct, it is best to survey each of them with a separate instrument.

The GM questionnaire should focus on the structure of the game, the intellectual debates in the context of learning outcomes and the playability of the game in the context of a course. The player questionnaire should focus on the role, comprehension of the texts and the historical context, as well as the factors that supported or hindered participation in the debates. If you distribute a questionnaire at a conference, it should be geared to capture impressions of the brief games; at this stage, you may be most interested in assessing the potential for course adoption. Finally, if you use preceptors, design questions for them as well. They have a valuable and unique perspective on the functioning of the games. In addition, since they are usually RTTP veterans, they are often well placed to compare your design to others they have played.[60]

When distributing questionnaires, encourage your reviewers to provide specific feedback and solutions to any problems they identify. Try to end with something upbeat like, "what was your favorite thing about this game?" If nothing else, these will make you feel good when you read through them.

The IM

In addition to the game materials, you need to write an instructor's manual. Often the last component to get written, many sections in the IM emerge from playtesting, but the sooner you begin sketching it out the better because the IM provides instructors what they need to administer the game *as GMs*.

---

[60] The initial inspiration for this section appears in Greenblat, 123, 125. Many thanks to John Moser, Jonathan Truitt, Kelly McFall, Bat Sparrow, and Mary Jane Treacy who provided substantial feedback on an earlier version of this section.

The IM also includes all privileged player information, which is disseminated by the GM, including the role sheets and a role assignment table, which allows GMs to balance the roles for classes of different sizes. If certain roles work best when played by people with specific character traits (vociferous, chatty, prompt, etc.) indicate that here.

The IM should also provide GMs with what they need to administer the game *as instructors*. A clear statement of your learning objectives should be foremost among these elements. These objectives should, in turn, inform the content of the reading prompts and discussion questions you provide for the opening days of traditional instruction. GMs also need notes for leading the debriefing discussion(s), which should include:

In addition, the IM should include information that allows instructors to administer the game *as scholars*. Elements of each of the following should already appear in the gamebook, but you may want to go into more detail in the IM.

Sources

Recognize that as an RTTP designer you are writing a genre of history. Like other works of history, a game develops a peculiar representation of the past. Consequently, you should remain just as conscious of your interpretative decisions as the author of any other historical work. Like a book, article, or museum display, your game is a unique conceptualization of the past, which will be conveyed to the people who play it.

If you conceal your interpretative decisions, your choices will be invisible to anyone who is not an expert when the game is played. Consequently, it can be quite helpful to include a short historiographical essay in either the gamebook or IM. In many cases this will be more an explanation of what you left out in order to make the game playable rather than what you put in to make the game accurate.

To assist these efforts, consider keeping an annotated bibliography. This will be helpful for you as a designer, and it will be even more helpful to future GMs and players. Keep this document open as the game evolves so you can continue dropping additional sources into it. Once you have a working prototype, you can use this master list as the basis for several elements of the game materials.

First, use it to develop a list of undergraduate-friendly recommended readings for your gamebook. Try to limit the books on the list to those that small college libraries can reasonably be expected to possess. They may then be put on reserve for the players. If you include electronic sources, find the most stable URL possible.

You can also use the whole document as an annotated bibliography for the IM in case GMs want to investigate certain topics in order to adapt the game to their particular needs. (Or, they may just be curious). Use your annotations to provide guidance to future GMs who are not experts in the area explored by the game. If they lack background knowledge, where should they seek it?

Designing for RTTP is as rewarding as it is demanding. So take a moment to ask, *why will people want to play my game?* Then ask, *what will they learn by playing my game?* Pose these questions early and often. Once you can answer them with confident assurance, keep them foremost in your mind and proceed.

In order to make sure you have all of the elements you need in your IM, please consult the following template. The *boilerplate* section on "Teaching RTTP" is shared by all of the games in the series (and it will be written soon). Naturally, each game may have peculiarities that may be addressed in this section as well.

Title Page
Table of Contents
Teaching RTTP *(Boilerplate)*
How to make this game your own
GM preparation for this particular game
    Learning objectives
    Key concepts
    Props (if any)
Model Schedules
    Schedule of sessions outline
    Various versions of schedules
Introducing the game
    Opening days
    Guidance for discussion
    Reading comprehension quizzes with keys
    Explanation for the function of different readings
Managing the game
    Rules and procedures
    Outline of necessary GM interventions (injections, etc.)
    Things to look out for (this section evolves in reaction to playtesting)
    Assignment checklist
    Managing the roles
        o   How the roles should interact
        o   Role allocation table(s)
        o   Role allocation questionnaire (optional)
        o   Resurrection policy (optional)
    Endgame procedures (optional)
    Objectives checklist
Guide to debriefing
    Learning objectives
    What actually happened?
    What happened next?

Why is this all important?

GM handouts (in the order they will need to be used)

Model assignments (with commentary)

Role Sheets

Recommended Reading

Mark Carnes, "Inciting Speech," *Change* (March/April 2005).

Mark Carnes, "Being There: The Liminal Classroom," *Chronicle Review* (Oct. 8, 2004).

Mark Carnes, "Setting Students' Minds on Fire," *Chronicle of Higher Education* (March 6, 2011).

Greg Costikyan, "I Have No Words & I Must Design." Originally published in *Interactive Fantasy* 2 (1994). Revised and published to the web at: http://www.costik.com/nowords2002.pdf.

Peter L. de Rosa, "Wargames in Introductory History Courses," *Academic Gaming Review*, vol. 5, no. 2 (Spring 2003): http://www.gis.net/~pldr/wihc.html.

Mary Flanagan, *Critical Play: Radical Game Design* (Cambridge, London: MIT Press, 2009).

Tracy Fullerton, *Game Design Workshop: A Playcentric Approach To Creating Innovative Games* (Amsterdam, Boston: Elsevier Morgan Kaufmann, 2008).

C. G. Greenblat, *Designing Games and Simulations: An Illustrated Handbook* (Newbury Park, CA: Sage Publications, 1987).

Mark D. Higbee, "How Reacting to the Past Games 'Made Me Want to Come to Class and Learn': An Assessment of the Reacting Pedagogy." In Jeffrey L. Bernstein, ed., *Making Learning Visible: The Scholarship of Learning at EMU* (Ypsilanti, MI: Eastern Michigan University, 2008).

Amanda Houle, "Reacting to 'Reacting,'" *Change* (July/Aug. 2006).

Johann Huizinga, *Homo Ludens: A Study of the Play Element in Culture* (Boston: Beacon Press, 1955).

Carsten Jessen, "Learning Games and the Disruptive Effects of Play" in *Serious Games in Education: A Global Perspective,* Simon Egenfeldt-Nielsen, et. al., eds. (Aarhus & Copenhagen: Aarhus University Press, 2011.

Raph Koster, *A Theory of Fun for Game Design* (Scottsdale: Paraglyph Press, 2005).

Tracy Lightcap, "Creating Political Order: Maintaining Student Engagement through *Reacting to the Past.*" *PS: Political Science and Politics* (2009), 42: 175-179.

Philip Sabin, *Simulating War: Studying Conflict through Simulation Games* (London: Continuum, 2012).

Katie Salen and Eric Zimmerman, *Rules of Play: Game Design Fundamentals* (Cambridge, London: MIT Press, 2004).

Birgitte Holm Sørensen, "Educational Design for Serious Games" in *Serious Games in Education: A Global Perspective,* Simon Egenfeldt-Nielsen, et. al., eds. (Aarhus & Copenhagen: Aarhus University Press, 2011.

Graham Walmsley, *Play Unsafe: How to work less, play harder and add stories to your game* (Lexington, KY: n.p., 2010).

For more readings see the "Selected Publications" page of the RTTP website: http://reacting.barnard.edu/news/publications

Acknowledgements

I hope this handbook is useful, but it is a dim candle beside the most valuable resource for designing games for RTTP: the Reacting community. My conversations and correspondence with other RTTP faculty about their experiences running and designing games permeate this work.

This community would not exist without Mark Carnes, so he deserves many thanks for coming up with the RTTP concept in the first place. His tireless efforts promoting, supporting, and refining RTTP and his apparently fathomless generosity are more impressive still, but these efforts would all be for naught without Dana Johnson. She is the Atlas upon which the whole enterprise rests.

Certain members of the community have been particularly helpful in arranging my thinking about game design. I've benefitted greatly from discussion on the RTTP Forum as well as the numerous face-to-face exchanges I've had with Jason Araujo, John Burney, Jonathan Coit, Elizabeth Dunn, Mark Higbee, Stephanie Jass, Heather Keaney, Paula Lazrus, Kelly McFall, John Moser, Adam Porter, Richard Powers, Joan Sitomer, David Stewart, Karmran Swanson, Mary Jane Treacy, Jon Truitt, and many others. Thanks to a Simpson College faculty development grant, I had the opportunity to visit a number of them on their home campuses for further conversation.

Playtesting is the key to developing good RTTP games, and in my experience they are also essential to developing an understanding of how games work. Eric Connon, Paul Fessler, Al Lacson, Bill Offutt, Bartholomew Sparrow, Jace Weaver, and Laura Weaver all greatly informed my thinking when they provided detailed feedback from playtests of my designs in their classes.

In terms of specific content, Pat Coby, Tony Crider, David Henderson, and Gretchen McKay provided especially useful comments on an early draft of the chapter game chapter. Megan Squire was instrumental in explaining the Creative Commons materials that appear above.

All of these people are great, but most of the ideas in this work emerged from conversations with my Simpson College history department colleagues Rebecca Livingstone and Judith Walden about our regular use of RTTP. Their work figuring out how to run games well has dramatically multiplied my experience with the day-to-day workings of these games in the classroom.

I've also learned about good game design from Justin Green and Karl Serbousek. They are dedicated and thoughtful gamers who provide excellent perspectives on gaming in general. The same is true of many participants in the 2010 Come Out and Play Festival. I had many interesting and insightful conversations over the course of a few short days. Andrew Ashcraft and Christopher Weed stand out in my memory as particularly thoughtful and generous.

My conversations with students who are particularly devoted to RTTP have continually reassured me that the future will be better after all; it rests in good hands. Jacqueline Chmielnicki, Maura Finn, Dani Holtz, Jessica Howell, Sumaiya Khalique, Vincent Massimino, Ellie Saxton, James Tatum, and Eric Welkos have all, to some extent, "majored in Reacting." They are sharp and inspiring, and I've enjoyed working with them all at a number of conferences.

As I noted in the introduction, I discovered most of what I know about game design as a result of trial and error. Consequently, students from (Simpson College) deserve particular thanks for the patience and good cheer with which they have endured my half-baked ideas and open-ended syllabi with notations like: *playtest until satisfied and/or exhausted.* Despite (or perhaps because of) this, my students regularly rise to the challenge. Eric Addy, Jennifer Arnold, Rawley Butler, Daphne Fernandez, Daniel Ginger, Leah Groethe, Derek Haugland, Ted Heying, Brandon Hyde, Laura Keller, Alex Koder, Maddy McAreavy, Dustin McNulty, Jordan Osborne, Mike Pearson, Adam Rademacher, Derrick Rodgers, Lara Roy, Scotty Schuknecht, Andrea Seehusen, Emily Stover, Allie Walker, and Tyson Wirtz, all deserve special recognition for pushing the potential of RTTP further than I thought it could go.

I particularly thank the students from my Historical Simulation Design seminars, which used early drafts of this work as a course reading. My experience facilitating the process of developing their outstanding prototypes – *Speak of the Devil: Hell-bent for Blood in Salem Village, 1692; America, the Great War in Europe, and Mexican Intervention, 1915-17; Revolution in the Heartland: The Farmers' Holiday Association, 1932-33, Vietnam: The Eve of Escalation, 1964-65; Chicago, 1968* and *Mary Queen of Scots* – greatly informed this most recent version.

These seminars certainly helped me refine my ideas about game design, but the best thing about them is that they gave me the opportunity to *play the games.* Students certainly made the most of it. As a consequence, I have been transported to re-education camp, imprisoned without trial, and pressed to death with heavy stones. Oh, how they cackled at that one. On the up side, I did get to initiate a milk riot, but as things turned out, this meant that I got beaten unconscious by hired thugs. However, I recently gained the Democratic nomination for president and wed Mary Queen of Scots, so things are looking up!

I like to pretend that it is work when I'm collaborating with gifted and devoted faculty to develop forthcoming designs for RTTP. Gretchen McKay and Michael Marlais (*Modernism vs. Traditionalism: Art in Paris, 1888-89*), Margaret Storey (*Kentucky, 1861*), and John Moser (*Yalta, 1945*), are great collaborators one and all, but working with them is not really work; it is play.

Finally, this little book is for James, Posy, and Christine, who constantly remind me that we play games for lots of reasons, but mostly because they are fun.

Des Moines, May 2013

15471619R00071

Made in the USA
Middletown, DE
07 November 2014